PRIOR PARK COLLEGE

THE PHOENIX

An Illustrated History

PETER CORNWELL

HALSGROVE

First published in Great Britain in 2005

British Library Cataloguing-in-Publication Data
A CIP record for this title is available from the British Library

ISBN 1 84114 455 X

Halsgrove House
Lower Moor Way
Tiverton, Devon EX16 6SS
Tel: 01884 243242
Fax: 01884 243325
email: sales@halsgrove.com
website: www.halsgrove.com

Printed and bound by CPI, Bath

Contents

	FOREWORD	4
	INTRODUCTION AND ACKNOWLEDGEMENTS	5
1	A PLACE WITH A VIEW	7
2	BATH'S CATHOLIC COMMUNITY	13
3	PETER AUGUSTINE BAINES	17
4	THE BIRTH OF PRIOR PARK COLLEGE	23
5	THE PHOENIX AFIRE	29
6	THE PHOENIX'S FIRST DEATH	35
7	THE RISE OF THE PHOENIX – THE DR WILLIAMS ERA	41
8	THE FIRST CHRISTIAN BROTHER ERA	51
9	THE RETURN OF THE CHRISTIAN BROTHERS	61
10	PRIOR PARK UNDER FIRE	75
11	THE POST WAR RECOVERY	89
12	NEGOTIATING A STRANGE NEW WORLD	109
13	THE FLICKERING PHOENIX	119
14	THROUGH TEMPEST AND FIRE INTO THE FUTURE	123
	BIBLIOGRAPHY	144

Foreword

A history of Prior Park is naturally of interest to all associated with it, but this particular story will appeal also to a wider readership: to those concerned with the history of education, especially Catholic education; to those who wish to explore an important avenue in the development of the Catholic community in this country; to those who want to know more about the history of Bath, its institutions, its architecture and its people. For all these and for others who simply want a thoroughly enjoyable book to read, Fr Peter Cornwell has provided an enriching and stimulating service.

Remarkably there are characteristics which have remained essentially the same at Prior Park from 1830 to the present. The first is the evident consensus of belief among the various bodies that have constituted the college, that the school community is only as good as the people in it, for better or for worse. As a comparatively small school this was true for all to see and, as a school which underwent closures, two fires and other vicissitudes, the 'phoenix' quality of Prior Park gave relief but it also concentrated minds. Survival could never be taken for granted. Change has had to be embraced again and again and so it has been, with courage and often far-sighted vision. Prior Park has often fostered a strong sense of community, while seeking to value the gifts of each individual. For a school of its size and without endowments or powerful patrons, Prior Park has almost from its inception tended to punch above its weight. At a deeper level the college has rooted itself in Catholic faith and drawn continuing vitality from it, reflecting in microcosm the changes undergone by the Catholic Church itself, from the immediate years following Catholic emancipation in 1829 and the establishment of the hierarchy in 1850 through to the strong winds of change of the Second Vatican Council in the 1960s and beyond. A deep practical commitment to ecumenism has emerged.

These strands are brilliantly interwoven in 'Phoenix' and full reign is given to some of the almost larger-than-life characters from Bishop Baines onwards. We encounter idealism, failure, love, faith and, at times, sheer comedy. The cast-list throughout the years plays against the same back-drop; the Palladian buildings of Ralph Allen's great villa, the meadows, flowers, birds, wild-life and stately trees which have fascinated so many of the young and their teachers from the start. The text and photographs evoke the natural and artistic beauty of Prior Park, *rus in urbe* of unsurpassed beauty.

Prior Park is most fortunate in having as its historian Fr Peter Cornwell, former chaplain and parent at the school and its abiding friend. I warmly commend 'Phoenix' to all readers.

Giles Mercer

Introduction and Acknowledgements

This is an attempt to tell the story of a Bishop's wild dream, which kept stubbing its toe on harsh economic realities and much else. Like the Phoenix the dream of Peter Augustine Baines, again and again, was to plunge to the earth in flames – both literally and metaphorically – and yet to keep rising again from the ashes. Of course, that Prior Park has won through is because it has been served by 'doers' as well as 'dreamers'. It has kept going by the faith of visionaries and the good works of the doggedly determined. What I have to offer here is but a portrait, not a definitive work. Br Roche's 1931 *History of Prior Park College*, despite the strictures of Downside when it was published, remains an indispensable guide to the college's early years. In order to tell a coherent story much fascinating material has had to be jettisoned and, in particular, I regret that I have been unable to make but passing references to the Prep School. This gap though has already been filled by Marion Parson's admirable *Story of Prior Park School*.

In fact the college is not over-generously endowed with archive material. There is valuable information to be found in the Clifton Diocesan Archive and I wish to thank the Archivist, the Rev. Dr J. A. Harding, for his kind assistance. Much more than I have written, could be said about how Prior Park got stuck in the mire of nineteenth century church politics, but I have resisted giving more than a taste of all this because what I have aimed for is the more human story of a school. I found myself asking all the time: 'What did it feel like to be a member of this community?' And to answer that question, it was necessary to ask: 'What was it like at that particular time?' Schools sometimes give the impression of floating timelessly above the real world, insulated from grave happenings around them. So I have turned to that remarkable source, the back numbers of the *Bath Chronicle*, made accessible in the City Library. There, stretching back into the eighteenth century, is a veritable treasure house of social history providing a vivid picture of the world into which Prior Park was born. I am grateful to patient librarians for their assistance in my struggles with the machines whereby readers have access to all this. But the real unsung heroes of my sources are all those editors of the school magazine over the years. The everyday happenings of school folk may not seem the most gripping of tales but through them the careful reader gets fascinating glimpses of what past generations were thinking. I came to this story wondering how in the 1930s the young saw the threat of the dictators in Europe, wondering how later a Catholic College viewed the upheavals in the Church set in motion by Pope John XXIII's Council. From school magazines I think I have got some answers.

I am grateful to Dr Giles Mercer for inviting me to embark on this venture, to Captain Charles Freeman and his staff in the Bursary for much assistance, and to former students at the college who have contributed both written recollections and photographic evidence of their days. Above all I am grateful to my dear wife Hilary for all her support which extends, beyond the encouragement of flagging spirits, to a sharp scrutiny of the text and many helpful suggestions. But in the end, of course, I must take responsibility for any errors of fact or judgement.

Many of our pupils, friends and staff have generously loaned photographs and given tremendous support for which we are extremely grateful. Particular thanks should go to Brian Warren-Peachey, Malcolm Upham, Brian Smith and Phil Hammerton.

Most grateful thanks go to Mrs Julie Barr, the Deputy Bursar of Prior Park College, for her sterling work, especially in regard to collecting and assembling photographs, which, as can be seen from the final product, was a major part of the enterprise.

Although at times it has been a labour, it really has been a labour of love. Both as a parent of a pupil at Prior Park and later as Chaplain, my affection and admiration for this community has grown over the years, so it is to the pupils and staff of Prior Park, past and present, that I dedicate this book – to all those boys and girls whose many gifts contribute to making the community such a civilized and friendly one I so much admire – and to all those members of staff whose hard work and dedication help this to happen.

Peter Cornwell

'I am delighted that the college has produced such a well-written book which helps to explain where the school is today. It brought back many memories. I recommend it warmly to all associated with Prior Park, to those interested in the development of the Catholic community in this country, to those concerned with the history of education – and to those who simply want a good book to read!'

His Eminence Cardinal Cormac Murphy O'Connor STL PhL

A PLACE WITH A VIEW

A teenage boy stands quietly looking out over a valley. It might seem a strange sight for the twenty-first century but indeed he stops and looks. If it is May he is rewarded by the yellow-greens of spring and the smell of all-pervading wild garlic. His eyes move, as they are meant to, down to the Palladian Bridge and beyond the ponds to the little church of St Thomas of Canterbury, with Widcombe Manor on its left and Crowe Hall on its right, and beyond that to the curvaceous crescents of Bath, with a glimpse of the Royal Crescent way out on the left and the solid squatting Abbey in the middle. All around are the hills encircling the city. If he is lucky the scene will be completed with the presence of cows in the valley and a buzzard hovering above. This is the landscape, which a former pupil of the College, the poet Peter Levi, called his father's 'mysterious gift ' to him. It is, wrote another pupil, 'an education in itself to look daily upon such sights as these.' This is not, of course, a book about a building or about a view but about the school, which inhabits that building and enjoys that view. But as all who have in any way passed through its life know, a sense of place is central to the Prior Park experience. So something must be said about the man who built this house and made this gift – Ralph Allen.

An early view from the steps of the Mansion, looking across the landscape gardens to Widcombe, and beyond to Bath.

The Palladian Bridge before restoration by the National Trust.

Ralph Allen, from a portrait which hangs at Prior Park.

The story therefore begins in the early eighteenth century down in Cornwall where the young Ralph worked in his grandmother's Post Office. A visiting inspector saw the lad at work and liked what he saw. As a result Ralph was to move from rural Cornwall to the up-and-coming city of Bath to be a clerk in the Post Office there. The eighteenth century was an era of patronage. If you wanted to ascend the ladder you needed someone at the top to give you a hand up. One day the sharp eyes of young Allen spotted amongst the post a subversive missive from a supporter of the Jacobite cause. Bath was in fact something of a centre for those who mourned the passing Stuarts and were unreconciled to the incoming Hanoverians. It was said that while the bell-ringers of the Abbey passed over the celebration of the accession of the current monarch, they still rang with enthusiasm for the birthday of James II. Quite what led Allen to be so suspicious of this item of post as to open it, we shall never know but it did him no harm for resident in Bath at this time was that scourge of the Jacobites, General Wade, and it was to him that the security conscious Allen passed the results of his intelligence gathering. The general was delighted, an erring cleric at the Abbey was arrested, and the young postal clerk's upward mobility was assured. Now he had a patron who would ensure his promotion to become Post Master of Bath. Alas the romantic post-script to this, that in addition Wade gave a daughter in marriage to Ralph Allen, is but a myth.

However, added to this helping hand, was undoubtedly Allen's sheer ability at his job. It was he who pioneered 'cross-posting', the system which enabled the post to move across the country more swiftly and from more places. It proved effective and very soon made Allen a wealthy man. He was proving not only a sharp spy but also an equally sharp business man for he negotiated a deal with the Post Office on highly favourable terms. It was with this newly acquired wealth that he purchased the stone quarries of Combe Down. Allen could see that up-and-coming Bath would mean a demand for houses and houses needed stone to be easily available. Just run a rail from the quarries down what is now called Ralph Allen Drive to the Dolmead Wharf by the River Avon which had just been opened up

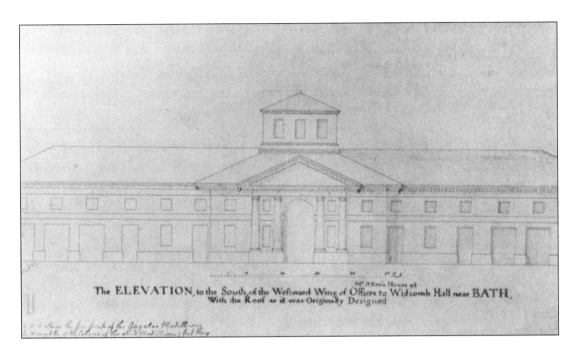

The ELEVATION, to the South, of the Westward Wing of Offices to Widcomb Hall near BATH, With the Roof as it was Originally Designed

The western wing of St Paul's, as designed by Wood and as it was after extension by Bishop Baines.

for navigation to Bristol and your stone is not only available for local use but can also be fed swiftly into the best available transport system. So, as well as your stone being used in Bath to build Queen Square and the Circus, you can hope for even greater things in London. But there was a fly in the ointment. It was put about that Bath stone was bad stone, as soft as that other product of Somerset, Cheddar cheese. 'That all depends, of course' replied Allen, 'on how skilful you are in treating and using it.' But he was also shrewd enough to know that one in the eye was worth any amount of persuasion poured in the ear – in other words that it paid to advertise his product. And so, on the hunting grounds of the old Prior of Bath, he planned the great mansion which would reveal to all Bath stone in its perfection and provide that view which can still capture the attention of youth. In 1735, the great although obsessive architect, John Wood, began to build. As he himself wrote: 'With natural terraces rising above one another like the stages of the seats of a Roman theatre; and on one of those terraces Mr Allen, one of the citizens of Bath, hath lately built himself a seat.' As is the way with architects and their clients not all was sweetness and light. Allen tinkered with Wood's plans and there was eventually a falling-out over the roof of the stables. The completion of the Mansion thus fell to the Clerk of Works, Richard Jones. Later Alexander Pope, the poet and landscape expert, would bring his vision to the surrounding grounds, to fashion cunning vistas and romantic ruins.

By the time Ralph Allen moved from his town house to Prior Park he had become something of a power in the city. As General Wade had given him a leg up, so now Allen was in turn to help the Member of Parliament for Bath, one William Pitt,

The tramway which was created to carry stone from the quarries to Bath, along what is now Ralph Allen Drive. This is taken from an engraving c 1760.

known to posterity as 'the Elder Pitt'. Indeed Allen's new mansion was to become a sort of court for up and coming interesting people. Here gathered not only the poet Pope, but also the actor Garrick, the novelist Fielding, and the ambitious ecclesiastic Warburton. Up at Prior Park, they said, you would find society refined and civilised, in stark contrast to the increasingly garish world of Beau Nash below.

The society, in which Allen's dream house was to become a College, was not only garish but also one which was living through a time of rapid change. The shadow or the bright hope, depending on how you saw it, of the French Revolution lay over all Europe. The thrones of kings were no longer secure, and established institutions, including the Church, felt threatened. Journalists wrote savagely about the glitzy privileged side of Regency England. Those in high and respectable places were nervous – yes even in Bath. The late eighteenth century sees the *Bath Chronicle* in a somewhat dark and apocalyptic mood. In 1778 the northern lights were said to have been 'more conspicuous than for years past.' It was an exceptionally hot dry summer with navigation on the Kennet and Avon canal impeded. What one wonders would have happened in this heat to the ladies who had responded to the *Chronicle* advertisement for 'Lady Molyneux's Italian Paste' to enamel the hands and face a lovely white. To cheer the spirits there was on 5 August in the Sydney Gardens the sixth 'musical entertainment in the style of London's Vauxhall', while Josiah Wedgwood 'opened rooms at Mr Ward's at the corner of Milsom Street to sell his china ware.' The year ended in some style with Captain Hartnell and Mr Lewis, the deputy Town Clerk, fighting a duel.

Whether your fancy turned to political revolution or not, there was no escaping the fact that the turn of the century saw something of a cultural change. There was in certain quarters a reaction to the conspicuous glitz and glamour that had been fashionable in the higher echelons of Regency society. This may have had something to do with the warning whiff of revolution from across the Channel but it had more to do with the great evangelical revival, associated not only with John Wesley but also William Wilberforce. Although, as we see from the circle in which Lord Byron moved, some of the great families continued to live it up in style, seriousness became fashionable and, as an outward and visible sign of it, wigs were abandoned and more sober dress was worn. But of course it all went deeper than that to the stirrings of social conscience. In Bath there was held a meeting to express concern about the fate of those clapped in gaol because of debt. Later the city was shocked by the story of a boy chimney sweep dying in a chimney. Of course it had all happened many times before but now regret turned to action, a meeting was called to attack 'the sweeping of chimneys by means of children.' It was not just the spirit of the age which was changing, the whole physical landscape of the nation changed with it by the revolution in communication that the railways brought. But that in itself brought more questions for the conscience. A sermon is preached at St Saviour's drawing attention to the sufferings of many railway workers as they worked the new line near Bath. Something the preacher believed must be done at least to alleviate their spiritual deprivation.

Way back in 1764 Ralph Allen had died, and after his death his great Mansion had passed through several hands until 1828 when once again it was up for sale. Notice was given of the forthcoming auction at a coffee house in London. This was the year when Mr Macready's performances as William Tell, Hamlet and Macbeth at the Theatre Royal, Bath, earned him 'plaudits' which the *Chronicle* critic rather crushingly held to be 'well intended but extravagant.' The *Chronicle*, for that year, seems to have been obsessed, as Charles Dickens was to be, by 'the fascinating possibility of the spontaneous combustion of the human body.' But under their noses there was quite a lot of social combustion in the city. There was great anxiety about the growing Chartist movement with its radical advocacy of the universal franchise and there is a note of nervousness in the mockery with which the *Chronicle* greets a forthcoming lecture in Bath on 'Socialism'! It was not just these political stirrings which generated fear but also issues of law and order. The *Chronicle* runs many grisly tales of violence and crime in the locality. Maria Bagnall was found murdered in Marlborough Buildings and there were accounts of highway robbery, sheep stealing and away near Aylesbury an armed robbery at a vicarage. To the perpetrators of all these crimes the death sentence was handed down. Grim details of public executions are given by the *Chronicle*, normally tinged with a concern about whether the criminal had passed to his death in a penitent frame of mind or not. At Winchester Moses Shepherd, aged twenty-three, was convicted for murder, executed and his body given to be dissected. This was the sort of world in which took place that sale of Prior Park which was to prove of such decisive importance to our story. But before we return to this we must consider the community that transformed an advertiser's dream into a college.

The tomb of Ralph Allen in the churchyard of Claverton Parish Church, Bath.

2

BATH'S CATHOLIC COMMUNITY

A society in which penal savagery mingled with signs of accelerating change – that was the sort of world into which Prior Park College was born. But it was, of course, also the world in which the Roman Catholic Church, from which the College was to spring, was slowly making its way. Slowly because for Catholics this was still a precarious world in which it was not yet quite accepted that they could be both faithful to their religion and loyal to their country. Way back on 15 November 1539 Abbot Whiting of the great Glastonbury Abbey, with two of his monks, was hanged, drawn and quartered on the Tor. One of those quarters was dispatched to be displayed in Bath to bring home to its citizens that now they had to choose between Pope and King. Choice for the former meant treason and attracted the appropriate penalties. There were to be other stories of heroic loyalty to the old religion like that of the Abbot and his monks, yet there are more, although less well advertised, stories of those who sought a way of being both faithful Catholics and accepted citizens. These stories of the search for quiet peaceable accommodation may be less colourful and dramatic, but they were still stories of lives not without considerable suffering for the faith. Such families who dissented from the worship of the Established Church and who struggled to practise their faith and educate their children in it, were often financially crippled by heavy fines.

Over the years the fires of popular anti-popery were stoked and prodded as the Church of England prayed in its Litany to be delivered 'from the Bishop of Rome and all his detestable enormities' and held annual thanksgiving on 5 November for the nation's escape from popish plotting. And yet on the ground, during the eighteenth century, toleration of Catholic worship, as long as it was discrete and

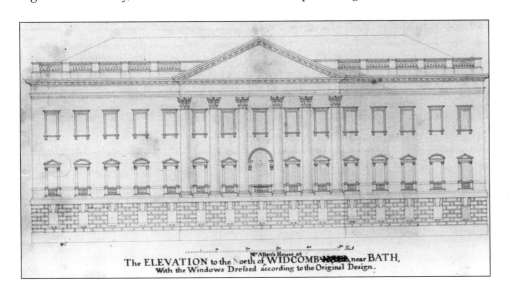

John Wood's original drawing of the house for Ralph Allen. Reproduced by kind permission of the Bath Library.

not flaunted, began to grow. Some forty years before the second Catholic Relief Act officially permitted such worship, the 1753 *Guide to Bath* quite openly mentions the Bell Tree Catholic Chapel. After all, as visitors began to flood to Bath to take the waters or to enjoy its social life, amongst those who came from overseas you could be sure that there would be Catholics, for foreigners had an unfortunate tendency to be Romanists rather than safely C of E. Bath's young tourist industry had to make sure that their peculiar religious needs were catered for. It was not only foreigners; at this time there came also members of eminent English Catholic families, the Fitzherberts, Throckmortons, Stonors and Vaughans. Sir Henry Bedingfeld, like many others, was a visitor for his health and although his wife spoke disparagingly of the 'nonsense and frivolity of Bath', they seem to have lived here a rich and full life, which, of course, included attending the Catholic Chapel. But it was not just the upper classes in search of the healthier life who came to Bath, there were waves of refugees from revolutionary France, and there is mention amongst the Catholic community of a German clock maker, several Italians, an Irish muffin man, and even a black African servant. It was indeed said that eighteenth century Bath was 'a veritable Mecca for Catholics'. Certainly between 1767-81 the number of Catholics in the city doubled.

The John Wood Chapel was constructed for the private use of Ralph Allen. It is now often used for lunchtime recitals and other events.

In a way therefore the Catholic Relief Act of 1778, allowing Roman Catholic priests to own property and be kept safe from persecution, simply confirmed what the citizens of Bath already allowed as it discretely advertised Catholic worship and, as memorials clearly show, laid Catholic dead to rest in the Abbey The Act required, in exchange for this degree of tolerance, an oath of loyalty to the crown. The Bath Chronicle, a somewhat happy hunting ground for anti-popish sentiment, described this as an 'ambiguous and insolent oath' even 'a lying oath' and records the uneasy Protestants of Bath declaiming:

'Hear us ye Gods of Britain! Hear us this day
Let us not fall the Roman Eagle's prey.
Clip, clip their wings and chase them home
And check the towering pride of Rome.'

These hard-line opponents of creeping toleration were eager to reassure readers that much of the old legislation remained firmly in place ' by which if any person shall put in practice to reconcile any subject to popery, or if any person shall be so willingly reconciled, he, his aides and maintainers, shall be guilty of high treason. And if any person, not bred a papist by his parents, shall breed up, or suffer his children to be bred up in the popish religion, so he shall be disabled from bearing any office till they conform.' The toleration of the late-eighteenth-century Establishment had its limits and was always vulnerable to resurgences of such anti-popery.

The most violent reaction to creeping toleration was that of the fanatical crazed Lord George Gordon who sparked off and gave his name to a particularly nasty

An early view of the Entrance Hall in the Mansion, looking through the double doors towards the John Wood Chapel.

burst of riots in 1780. On 9 June of that year Bath had its share of these troubles. John Butler a footman employed by the Baldwins in the Royal Crescent, while serving at table heard guests bewailing Bath's lack of spirit in not imitating the rioters of London in their anti-Catholic zeal. Responding, as Henry II's knights were said to have responded to the sovereign's complaints about Becket, Archbishop of Canterbury, Butler left his work full of that zeal which was said to have been so lacking in Bath, and joined by a one-eyed milkman, quickly gathered a mob. To the stirring sound of fife and drum they advanced upon 'the elegant Roman Catholic chapel, lately built, near St James's Parade.' The mob eagerly sacked and burned the chapel along with the six or seven adjoining buildings that were known to be in Catholic ownership. They then spotted the unfortunate priest Father Brewer. He took to his heels and pursued by the mob, fled via the Abbey to the Guildhall where he sought assistance. None was forthcoming but the good Father was to find sanctuary eventually at the nearby White Lion Inn, an hostelry thereafter to be frequented and honoured by Catholics in Bath. In all the ensuing mayhem and confusion, the mob managed to throw over the wall into St James's churchyard an unfortunate man who, they claimed 'must be the Pope because he lodged in St James's Parade and had a night-gown with gold flowers on it'! All the time the mob grew. It was joined by unruly elements from outside the city, particularly, they said, from the nearby mining districts. Now the civic authorities were not only embarrassed but also alarmed. The Bath Volunteers were mustered, the Riot Act read and more troops were summoned, the Queen's Dragoons began to march from Devizes and others from Wells. The Guildhall carried a 'Wanted' notice, signed by the Mayor and the Justices, for 'a Twenty-three year old man with a patch over one eye – employed carrying milk sought for setting fire to the Roman Catholic chapel.' Justice, when it caught up with him,

was swift and harsh. He was sentenced at the Taunton Assizes and hanged in Bath. Perhaps the Catholic community found greater satisfaction in the Court's award of three thousand pounds in damages.

Each step taken towards toleration of the Catholic community seems to have been punctuated by outbursts of almost ritual anti-Catholicism. Bath saw the publication of pamphlets with such colourful titles as 'The Protestant Alarm or Popish Cruelty Fully Displayed' which were aimed to stir up resistance to further relief for Catholics. As late as 1828 we read in the *Chronicle* warnings of the 'dangers of admitting Roman Catholics to Parliament'. That would be to admit 'the enemy into the citadel of our strength.' 'Beware men of England! Concessions have gone too far!' The clergy of the Archdeaconry of Bath voted 40 –1 against further relief for Catholics while Sir Ralph Inglis presented a petition signed by 5806 citizens to the same effect. Sir Thomas Lethbridge judged that 'the feelings of the people of Bath were decidedly hostile to the Catholic question' but that was challenged by a counter petition supporting Catholic relief presented by a Mr Brownlow and signed by nine clergymen, presumably from other nonconforming churches, forty army and naval officers and one hundred tradesmen – the latter no doubt realizing that their bread was as much buttered by papists as by Protestants.

Despite rearguard resistance, toleration seems to have been remorselessly growing. There is nothing of Protestant panic when the *Bath Chronicle* advertises a great High Mass 'at the Catholic Chapel on Thursday next' to the accompaniment of the music of Haydn and Mozart. Thus, with a sermon advertised on the Real Presence of Christ in the Mass, was the feast of Corpus Christi openly and calmly celebrated. When next an ecclesiastic was set upon by the mob in Bath, it was in 1831 and that was in the belief that he was one of those prelates of the Established Church who had just voted against the Reform Bill. The fact that this Bishop of Cork who was tumbled out of his carriage turned out to be, not a bishop of the establishment but the Catholic bishop was just hard luck! By this time anti-clericalism had taken an ecumenical turn.

Through all such vicissitudes Lady Bedingfeld recorded the life of a lively Catholic community. There were the two Miss Ferrars 'the eldest not young, very sensible and pleasing; the other cracked.' There in 1809 was Madam Catalini singing the Agnus Dei in the chapel 'a most interesting woman, pensive and naive' though her husband was dismissed as 'an ugly Frenchman, vulgar.' Priests supplied by the Benedictine Abbey of Ampleforth came and went. In 1814 Fr Ainsworth died and was succeeded by Fr Calderbank. It was one of his assistants Fr Clement Rishton who seems to have become somewhat over friendly with a Bath governess with whom he continued to correspond after he had left the city. A few years later they got married.

3

PETER AUGUSTINE BAINES

In 1817 there came from Ampleforth to the Pierrepont Place Chapel in Orchard Street the new Bath Missioner, Peter Augustine Baines, with his assistant Thomas Brindle. Baines burst in on the Bath scene with some vigour and like many another priest was suspected of being rather 'new broomish'. He certainly displayed a trait, which was later to get him into trouble – he knew how to spend money and that lavishly. It often seemed that investment in Divine Providence was treated as a substitute for investment in the Bank. This spending was not, of course, on himself. The Catholic community owned quite a lot of property and it was sadly in bad repair so Baines, in remedying this, was simply being a good steward. He also cared deeply for the fabric of the chapel and its furnishings. Everything had to be to a high standard. A new organ was installed, a more than competent choir assembled and Baines himself always took the greatest of care with his preaching. It was said that he himself was often moved to tears by his own homilies – before ever the congregation was! But he proved to be much more than an efficient administrator and a liturgical perfectionist. He busied himself with the bread and butter work of a parish priest – spent long hours in the confessional, was always out and about visiting his flock and presided over what seems to have been a very large number of funerals. One suspects that funerals took up a great deal of all the clergy's time in Bath for many of the pilgrims to the city were sickly pilgrims in search of healing waters which clearly did not always work.

Although Baines was more than ready to take on the redoubtable Archdeacon Moyser in ecclesiastical debate, he was one of those old Catholics who sought quiet accommodation and so was careful not to exaggerate differences or make his flock stick out like a sore thumb. Catholics, he believed, should fit into Bath and seek to serve its life so he was careful to see that the Orchard Street Chapel made its proper contribution to the Bath Hospital and the Dispensary. By nature he was a gregarious man and chose to dine, not just amongst his co-religionists, but amongst all and sundry. As a lover of good music he clearly enjoyed popping into the Abbey to attend a performance of Handel's *Messiah*. Baines believed and taught that Catholics could be both true to their faith and fully a part of British life. His advice to new priests exalted the virtues which would make this possible: 'Be pious, be learned, be gentlemanlike and not less than any of these be quiet, plain-dealing, honest upright fellows.'

Baines was not to be left long as the Bath Missioner. His bishop of the Western District, Peter Collingridge, was in poor health and so sought a co-adjutor bishop,

Bishop Baines, from a portrait at Prior Park College.

an Episcopal assistant who would have the right of succession. For this his eyes lighted on the clearly able Peter Augustine Baines. Such was his recommendation to Rome. It was accepted and in 1832 the Bath Missioner was consecrated bishop. Now Baines came to this task with a sharply clear agenda. He had an understanding of the changes which must be embraced as the Catholic Church emerged from hiding onto the public scene and had to handle its new freedoms. Under persecution it had existed in a necessarily hand-to-mouth sort of way with but a rough and ready organization. Priests as men on the run needed to be sturdily independent. Penal times bred resilient individualism. In recent years the growth of practical toleration had allowed the re-emergence of the episcopate – with bishops presiding over four districts. But there was as yet no diocesan structure with a clear chain of command. Catholic communities were 'missions' many of them, as in Bath, under the control of the religious orders rather than a bishop. Bath was Benedictine land but Baines, himself of course a Benedictine monk, believed that if bishops were to be bishops they needed to be able to control their own manpower. If the bishop were to control the mission in his district, he must not have to depend on a supply of priests from the religious orders, but have an assured supply of his own and that meant setting up and controlling a chain of education and training. So each district needed a seminary to train priests and a school to feed the seminary – perhaps even its own university.

There is a somewhat modern ring about Baines's insight that the foundation of success should be 'education, education, education.' He was no amateur in the world of education for he had been himself an inspired and successful teacher in the school at Ampleforth. There he had become a convinced disciple of the newly fashionable Feinagle system which should again resonate with modern teachers for it laid emphasis on constant testing of pupils and the provision of public examinations. Even before his consecration as bishop there was brewing in the mind of Baines a Prior Park- shaped vision and on accepting the post of bishop coadjutor, he wrote: 'I shall omit no opportunity that may offer prudently to prepare the way for procuring a college for the district.'

A view of the College from the Palladian Bridge. Plunder from Ampleforth included a herd of cows and cattle graze on the hillside to this day.

How now was the vision to become reality? Baines, like many bishops before and after, came face to face with the limitations of episcopal power. He would have liked the dream to be realised by his Benedictine brethren and to that end he bent his mind and their backs. His own monastery up in Yorkshire was too far to be of much use but perhaps Ampleforth might be persuaded to provide some foot soldiers for the enterprise and itself give up its educational work so that it could be concentrated in the Western District. But where would the site for that be? Downside might be suitable but it was rather tucked away in the country. Yet all these musings and plans came up against the fact that Baines had no control over either community. Religious orders cherish their independence and do not like to be pushed around by bishops even if, or perhaps especially if, the bishop happens to be a fellow Benedictine. Within the community your abbot might be a tyrant and give you all a rough ride but when he came up for re-election as he must, you could always get rid of him. Not so with bishops. You are stuck with them – usually until death – yours or his!

Particulars of sale for the Prior Park Estate in 1828. The sale included the quarries. The original document is held by the school.

In the end the monks of neither Ampleforth nor Downside wanted to be controlled by Peter Augustine Baines. Men of such single-minded determination that it can be called 'tunnel vision' may turn out geniuses or even saints but they are suspected by their contemporaries and, if saints, often end up as martyrs. Nor was it quite clear how attached Baines really was to the Benedictine way of life. He was an individualist rather than a member of a community. He seems to have sat lightly to that round of prayer and worship, the Opus Dei, to which Benedict summoned his brethren. On the contrary Baines claimed that Pope Gregory had dispatched the Benedictines to this land, not to be 'mere contemplatives' but to spearhead the Church's mission. On this view monks should be out of their monasteries and into the parishes. When, on his consecration in 1823, he sent a final proposal to both monasteries that they should throw in their lot with 'an Episcopal seminary in the neighbourhood of Bath', while Burgess of Ampleforth seemed mildly encouraging, Barber of Downside said a blunt 'No'. At this early stage the new bishop made it clear that he would not easily take this for an answer. 'They are not aware' he ominously wrote 'how strenuous and efficient my opposition to them will be if they drive me into it.'

No sooner had Baines become a bishop and gone to live in Bathampton, than he was struck down with illness. Doctors advised that he should take himself off from the unhealthy environs of Bath to sunnier parts. So in 1826 he set off for a very leisurely trip to Rome – an excursion which was to take all of three years. The journey itself included time spent in France where the bishop did not find Church music to his taste. 'The yells and bellowings made for the honour and glory of God in French churches' he concluded 'are perfectly torturing.' Once in Rome at least the music improved. Singing in St Peter's

Somerset, Prior Park, near Bath.

CAPITAL FAMILY STONE-BUILT MANSION,
With Offices of every description,
COTTAGE ORNEE, FARM HOUSE, AND LANDS,
NEARLY TWO HUNDRED ACRES,
With Quarries of Bath Free Stone, of the finest Quality.

Particulars and Conditions of Sale,
OF A VALUABLE
LEASEHOLD ESTATE,
(Tithe Free,)
HELD FOR
A TERM OF ABOUT EIGHT HUNDRED YEARS,
(WITH PART FREEHOLD,)
COMPRISING
A capital and substantial Mansion,
PRIOR PARK,
IN THE PARISH OF
LYNCOMB AND WIDCOMB, ABOUT ONE MILE FROM THE CITY OF BATH,
Formerly the Residence of the Right Hon. LORD HAWARDEN, and erected, in the most substantial manner, about the Year 1738, by RALPH ALLEN, Esq.
SEATED ON AN EMINENCE, WITH EXTENSIVE TERRACE WALK IN FRONT,
Commanding highly interesting and beautiful Prospects in various directions, to a great extent.
THE MANSION
IS PLANNED FOR THE ACCOMMODATION OF A NOBLEMAN, OR FAMILY OF DISTINCTION,
And contains numerous well-proportioned Apartments,
A GRAND HALL IN THE CENTRE,
A Beautiful Chapel,
A MAGNIFICENT PORTICO IN FRONT,
DOMESTIC OFFICES OF ALL DESCRIPTIONS IN THE BASEMENT,
Stables, Coach Houses,
ARCHED GRANARIES, AND SERVANTS' APARTMENTS OVER, RENDERED FIRE-PROOF,
THE WINGS ARE IN UNISON,
AND CONTAIN OTHER OFFICES FOR DOMESTIC PURPOSES;
ALSO,
A Beautiful and Compact Residence,
ELEGANTLY FITTED UP, AND A CONSERVATORY,
A SPACIOUS CARRIAGE DRIVE ON THE SOUTH-FRONT OF THE MANSION,
And Park-like Grounds, ornamented with an Obelisk,
A GRAND TERRACE WALK ON THE PRINCIPAL FRONT,
The Grounds forming a very beautiful Dell, skirted on each side with Trees of great variety, size, and beauty,
A PALLADIAN BRIDGE OVER A FINE SHEET OF WATER,
Constantly fed from various Streams, intersecting the Grounds;
A COTTAGE ORNEE,
With GARDEN, &c., from which there is most enchanting Scenery,
A CAPITAL RANGE OF GARDEN GROUND,
Walled and Cross Walled, clothed with choice Fruit Trees.
THE GROUNDS
ARE RICHLY ADORNED WITH THRIVING TIMBER AND EVERGREENS, EXTENSIVE WALKS AND RIDES,
A Grotto, Alcove, and Cascades;
PRIOR PARK FARM HOUSE,
WITH MEADOW AND PASTURE LAND,
CONTAINING, TOGETHER, NEARLY
TWO HUNDRED ACRES:
WHICH WILL BE SOLD BY AUCTION,
BY MR. ROBINS,
OF WARWICK HOUSE, REGENT STREET,
AT GARRAWAY'S COFFEE HOUSE, 'CHANGE ALLEY, CORNHILL,
On THURSDAY, the 10th of JULY, 1828, at Twelve o'Clock,
By Order of the Executors and Devisees in Trust, and by Direction of the late Mr. JOHN THOMAS, Deceased.
QUARRIES OF BATH FREE STONE,

CONDITIONS OF SALE.

I. THAT the highest Bidder shall be declared the Purchaser; and if any Dispute shall arise between two or more Bidders, the Estate shall be immediately put up again.

II. That no Person advance less than Twenty Pounds at each Bidding.

III. The Purchaser shall pay down immediately, into the Hands of Mr. ROBINS, a Deposit of Fifteen Pounds per Cent. in Part of the Purchase-Money, and sign an Agreement for Payment of the Remainder, on or before the 29th Day of September, 1828, upon having a good Title, as after mentioned. All Out-goings will be cleared to that Time.

IV. The Purchaser shall have a proper Conveyance of the Freehold, and an Assignment of the Leasehold (at his own Expense), on Payment of the Remainder of the Purchase-Money, agreeably to the Third Condition. Possession will be given on the Completion of the Purchase.

V. That an Abstract of the Title shall be delivered to the Purchaser; and if the Completion of the Purchase shall be delayed after the 29th Day of September, 1828, the Vendors shall be entitled to Interest on the Purchase-Money and Valuation of the Timber, &c., at the Rate of Five Pounds per Cent. per Annum.

VI. That inasmuch as the Vendors deduce their Title from RALPH ALLEN, Esq., who died in 1764, the Purchaser shall not require the Production of the Deeds creating the several Terms of One Thousand Years, commencing in or about the Year 1593, or either of them, nor any further or more Ancient Title than the Title from the said RALPH ALLEN, Esq. All Attested Copies of Deeds, and other Documents required by the Purchaser, shall be had at the Expense of the Person requiring the same.

VII. The Timber, Timber-like Trees, Tellers, Pollards, Saplings, and other Trees, down to Two Shillings and Sixpence per Stick, and that inclusive, growing upon the Estate, shall be taken at a Valuation by the Purchaser, and paid for over and above, and at the same Time with, the Residue of the Purchase-Money agreed to be paid at this Sale; such Valuation to be made by two indifferent Persons (one to be chosen by the Vendors and the other by the Purchaser); and in case they cannot agree in their Valuation on or before the 12th Day of September, 1828, [...] former two, whose Valuation shall [...] of such two Persons, or such one [...]

VIII. The Auction-Duty of Seven Pence [...]

IX. If, through Mistake, any Article is [...] not vitiate the Sale, but the Purc[...] portionate Value, according to th[...] way.

Lastly, Upon Failure of complying with [...] of the Time before limited) becom[...] without Notice, or tendering any [...] should be any Deficiency, the P[...] shall make good such Deficiency [...]

Printed by [...]

7

Reference to Plan.		A.	R.	P.
	Brought forward	149	1	9
No. 28. New Plantations and Road	plantation	1	3	16
29. The West Lawn	pasture	11	1	37
30. Upper Lodge and Garden	pasture	0	0	9
31. The Beeches	plantation	17	3	0
32. Plantation	plantation	0	2	0
33. Rookery	pasture	15	3	22
34. Private Carriage Road		1	3	15
	TOTAL	198	2	28

OUT-GOINGS:

	£.	s.	d.
Nos. 19 and 20, 31 and 32, containing 27A. 2R. 6P. are Freehold, and are subject to certain Rents, payable to the Trustees to the Hospital at Bruton, amounting together to, per Annum	5	12	8
The remainder is Leasehold, for several Terms of One Thousand Years, commencing in or about the Year 1593, and are subject to small Quit Rents, amounting together to, per Annum	1	16	5.
Land Tax, per Annum	6	18	10
Hoggen Flock Rent	0	18	9
	£.18	6	6

QUARRIES OF BATH FREE STONE,

OF CONSIDERABLE EXTENT, & OF THE FINEST QUALITY,

Might be worked in a very lucrative way.

BEING ONLY

ONE MILE FROM BATH, AND THE KENNET AND AVON CANAL,

By which Stone may be easily conveyed to London, where it has been used in many of the Public and other Buildings, and is now in great demand.

THE BRADFORD ROAD PASSES THE WEST SIDE

OF THE QUARRIES.

A line of Road has been projected, rising at an inclination of Two Inches in the Yard, from near the Rock Gate, marked A, to the summit B, and shown by a dotted line on the Plan, of a Mile in length, which presents very advantageous Sites for Building, whereby the Property may be rendered highly lucrative.

Particulars of sale for the Prior Park Estate in 1828.

Somerset, Prior Park, near Bath.

PARTICULARS AND CONDITIONS OF SALE,
Of a Valuable

LEASEHOLD ESTATE,

(Tithe Free,)

Held for a Term of about Eight Hundred Years,
(WITH PART FREEHOLD,)
Comprising

A capital & substantial Mansion,

PRIOR PARK,

In the Parish of LYNCOMB and WIDCOMB, about One Mile from the City of BATH;

THE MANSION

Is planned for the Accommodation of a Nobleman, or Family of Distinction,

A beautiful and compact Residence,

ELEGANTLY FITTED UP,

And PARK-LIKE GROUNDS, ornamented with an OBELISK;

A COTTAGE ORNEE,

With Gardens, &c. from which there is most enchanting Scenery,

THE GROUNDS

Are richly adorned with thriving Timber and Evergreens, extensive Walks and Rides,

A GROTTO, ALCOVE, AND SEVERAL CASCADES;

PRIOR PARK FARM HOUSE,

WITH MEADOW & PASTURE LAND,

CONTAINING NEARLY

TWO HUNDRED ACRES;

WITH

QUARRIES OF BATH FREE STONE:

which will be Sold by Auction,

of the Executors and Devisees in Trust, and by [...] on of the late Mr. JOHN THOMAS, Deceased,

MR. ROBINS,

[...]raway's Coffee House, 'Change Alley,
CORNHILL,

[...]SDAY, the 10th of JULY, 1828,

At Twelve o'Clock.

[...]reet.

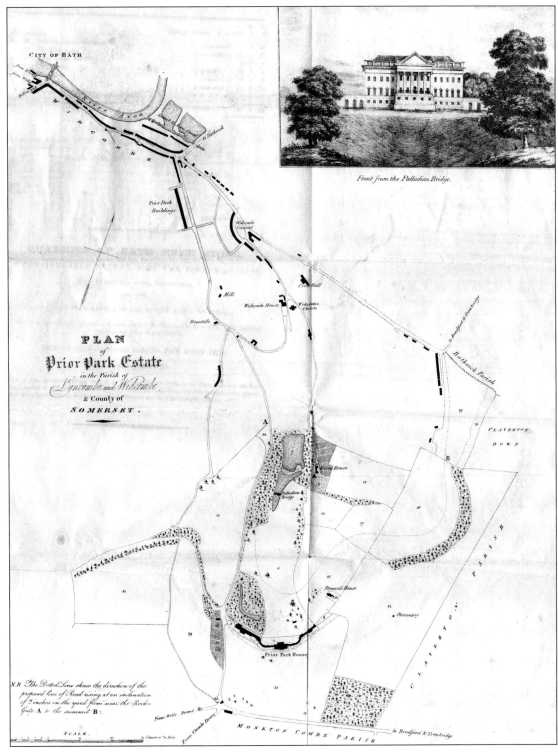

Front from the Palladian Bridge.

Particulars of sale for the Prior Park Estate in 1828.

conveyed 'the idea of heaven.' But while Baines lived it up in Rome, back in Bath his old assistant at Pierrepont Place, Father Brindle, who had now become the Missioner, kept him in touch with local developments. It was from Brindle in 1828 that Baines received the news that Prior Park was once more for sale. The Mansion, its surrounding buildings, and 198 acres of land were to be auctioned with a reserve price of £35,000. What could better serve the bishop's grand educational vision? thought Brindle. Baines clearly warmed to the idea and still 'vowing not to submit to the insolence of the Downside faction', yet seemed in no haste to rush back home and seize the reins of power. In 1829 Pope Leo XII died and the lure of a papal funeral followed by the excitements of the election of a new pope, held Baines in Rome. There was still time in August to go to Florence for the races on the feast of St Laurence.

It was not until mid September that he returned to England. The weather conditions in London were truly depressing. From the sunshine of Italy he was plunged into 'a climate, which seemed composed of mist, smoke and hurricane.' After 'the warmth, the wide airy streets, the vineyards and olive groves, it distressed my spirits exceedingly.' The last straw was a visit to St Paul's cathedral where, having paid two pence to enter, he found the aisles and nave 'actually barricaded with rails.' It seemed a sign of all the barriers and impediments which were to stand in the way of the realisation of his dreams.

THE BIRTH OF PRIOR PARK COLLEGE

That same year Bishop Collingridge had died so Baines was now coming home as the new Bishop of the Western District. The reins were finally in his hands and he soon made his presence known as he cracked the whip over his opponents at Downside. But he did this in the most ill-advised way. Baines played the barrack-room lawyer, claiming that their monastery had not been set up in a duly canonical way; all of which meant, he said, that their vows were null and void, and that therefore all these priests came under the bishop's control. To make this point forcibly clear, he withdrew Downside's missionary faculties and so effectively undermined their parish work. It was a stupid bit of canonical nit-picking. In no way could the correct requirements have been fulfilled under the conditions of penal times. The case was to be argued in Rome where it was concluded that if the strict law was on Baines's side, common sense and justice were on the side of the Benedictines. However that judgement lay in the future; for the present the Baines juggernaut moved on its way. The Bishop of the Western District purchased Prior Park for £22,000 which, considering the reserve price had been set at £35,000, was even then a bit of a bargain. Now the way was opened for the College to be established. If Baines had failed to plunder Downside, he had more success with Ampleforth. There he caused something of a schism in the community, managing to entice the Prior, Burgess, the Sub Prior, Rooker and the Procurator, Metcalfe, to leave their monastery to staff his new college. Along with the monks came three dozen boys as pupils, the housekeeper, a portrait of St Jerome and a herd of cows. All this plunder was to be the cause of further dissension, a mounting file in Rome and the demonisation of Baines in Benedictine communities.

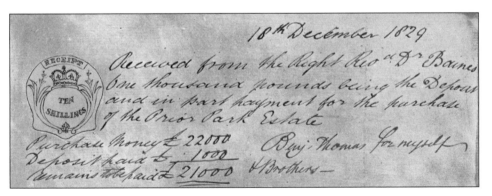

Receipt for the Prior Park Estate given to Bishop Baines.

On 1 May 1830 the Bishop was able to take possession of Prior Park. The *Bath Chronicle* darkly spoke of a 'formidable rival to Protestant colleges'. Archdeacon Moysey holding his visitation at the Abbey expressed apprehension at this 'immense establishment' and called on ministers of the Church of England to 'exercise increased vigilance to counteract its influence.' A prospectus announced

An early view of the rear of the Mansion looking towards St Peter's.

Prior Park as a community of two distinct establishments – the one St Peter's College, a school for junior students and the other St Paul's College for 'students of more advanced age and acquirements.' While students in the former slept 'in separate beds but not separate rooms', the latter had private bedrooms and ate with the 'superiors and professors.' Each student in St Peter's had to come armed 'with a silver fork and spoon.'

The two colleges were soon up and running. In June of the following year it could make its mark with an open air Corpus Christi procession in the grounds and follow this up with an 'exhibition' or public display of the progress of students. This event which was a sort of cross between Speech Day and an Open Day was to become a feature of the establishment. The great and the good of Bath would assemble to witness some notable personage firing questions at pupils. The story is told of Mr Kavanagh's class successfully fielding the questions of Lord Clifford. For over an hour he quizzed them on 'Hannibal's campaigns, Caesar's conquests, Popes, General Councils, Crusades, Goths and Burgundians.' Pupils, it was said, 'with eager hands uplifted' competed to fire back the answers, until Lord Clifford threw in the sponge and declared himself beaten! Thunderous was the applause given to the winners of this contest. The guests then witnessed the beginning of Prior Park's tradition of drama with productions of both *Julius Caesar* and *Le Bourgeois Gentilhomme*.

It all got off to a good enough start but the limitations of centralised episcopal control soon became apparent. Baines had taken up residence in the college, a highly visible sign of the importance he attached to this enterprise. His was a hands-on approach but he liked to paint with a broad brush leaving the necessary detail to be inserted in an ad hoc way. So there was a flow of verbal instructions from the resident prelate which alas often conflicted with one another leaving his colleagues in a right old muddle. The staff rebelled and, as a body, threatened resignation if clarity and order could not be delivered. Baines's response was both lengthy and exhaustive in a painstaking document. Everything seemed to be there – including the use of corporal punishment, which, in the light of some later periods of the college's history, seems liberal and enlightened. Such punishment, the bishop believed, 'ought to be reserved to brute creatures where there is no reason to guide, no moral or religious principles to restrain' so it may be only used 'in cases where the student acts as a brute and is insensible to rational correction.' As a mark of this disdain for physical punishment, Baines decreed that, if it was necessary, it should yet be inflicted 'not by a master but by a servant or drill sergeant.'

We are fortunate in having a lively picture of what life at Prior Park was like in those early days from L. Guibara's *Reminiscences of James Kavanagh*, the member of staff whose class had outwitted Lord Clifford. Known affectionately as 'old Jem', he was said to have been 'unfitted for female society' and had 'a blind hatred of rules and regulations.' Despite, or because of the latter, he was a civilized and wise schoolmaster; his presence in the junior house St Peter's is said to have 'soft-ened its Spartan hardness'. Like many another teacher of that time, and of times considerably later, old Jem had a go at teaching a bit of everything which included French, a language of which he is said to have known little. But, as it turned out, he proved to be a better teacher of it than was the imported Abbé Lorraine whose native tongue it was – perhaps another example of how learners often prove to be better teachers than experts. It was somewhat the same with botany for which also Kavanagh's zeal was greater than his knowledge. He loved to show the boys the trees around Prior Park and to take them on long nature rambles. All this he would do armed with an old manual which contained the information on trees. He would stop, sit down under a great beech tree and consult this volume with loving care. Invariably on a warm afternoon he would drop off to sleep, leaving his charges to have the time of their lives. Yet something of the teacher's passion-ate love for the trees and flowers rubbed off on at least some of those boys. Young Guibara himself was amongst them and acquired a life-long zeal for the study of flora and fauna. It was he who listed the remarkable variety of wild flowers in the college grounds and warned of the advent of the 'dreadful garlic' whose advance would destroy so much of this. Even back in 1887 we find Guibara arguing that wild flowers needed protection by the law.

Old Jem showed more of his all-round ability as a teacher in the bathing expedi-tions he led to the river at Monkton Combe. 'Valour! Valour!' he would cry to the boys, 'Shall I stand lingering, shivering on the brink?' And with these words he would plunge into the river. As the lads were enticed to imitate him, some began to sink and then it was old Jem to the rescue. He is said to have saved the life of one Henry Segrave. However, being saved by Kavanagh seems to have been almost as uncomfortable as being drowned for he believed that the way to 'restore animation' was the throw the luckless victim into a bed of stinging nettles! But perhaps they revived, as on the journey back to the college from Monkton Combe, Kavanagh would stop to purchase huge fresh loaves of bread to be eagerly gobbled by the young swimmers. He was, in all ways, a gentle man with a sharp eye for bullying and quick to restrain what he called 'ruffianism'. He was ever ready to come to the defence of pupils whom other staff condemned and was always working to blunt the sharp edge of school discipline and indeed slyly to subvert the regime when it seemed to become too harsh and rigorous. And yet, in all this, he was the most devoted and loyal of the supporters of Bishop Baines for he believed that it was Baines himself who had humanized ' the semi-barbarous system which our colleges had pursued' and Baines who had seen that school rules should be a means to 'moral expansion, not merely a means of juvenile repression.'

The Ball Court.

The Ball Court and Gymnasium before English Heritage assisted with the restoration.

No account of school life seems complete without some sporting tales. Competing with other schools was at this stage unknown to Prior Park – here the emphasis was on fun, frolic and physical exercise for home consumption. Old Jem was always trying to wangle extra playtime for the boys. It was said that, among Catholic schools, Prior Park was long characterised by a 'wild enthusiasm for ball playing.' This seems to be a reference to a variety of Fives played in the much-loved Ball Court. Apart from this there was a bit of rather rough and ready cricket and a type of football which seems to have been innocent of almost all rules and unique to Prior Park – as were also games called 'Bandy' and 'Hawney Holes', the latter a most complex form of rounders, the details of which the writer has studied and totally failed to comprehend. Kavanagh kept a wary eye to make sure that the smaller boys of St Peter's were not edged off the field by the 'sporting giants' but there was 'no shrinking or sleeping at your post possible when he was within reach'. 'His shouts of victory whenever we beat the Paulites' wrote Guibara 'were as delicious to our ears as Napoleon's praises were to his troops after a hard battle.'

Baines, who had nurtured church music at the Pierrepont Place Chapel, shuddered at French choirs and been captivated by the singing in Rome, was now to ensure that the foundations of musical excellence were laid at the college. All at the Bishop's expense, Mr Manner the music master was dispatched to Rome to study under the best composers. When he returned to Prior Park he came with new skills and many musical treasures. Baines took a personal interest in the development of the college's musical life. He was to be seen watching 'our elaborate rehearsals' from the gallery at the back of the John Wood Chapel. Henry Field was to take the music to new heights before a sadly early death. It was he who on his deathbed cried to a colleague: 'Sing to me John – sing our Lady's Litany.' Later in the century Signor Rivalli introduced the College to selections of Verdi operas. It was said that he 'did so much to keep up love of music till his mind gave way and he had to be placed in an asylum' thus giving a warning message to subsequent directors of music who might be tempted towards the cultivation of eccentricity.

Baines continued to be as careful about the quality of music and ceremonial in the chapel as he had been at Pierrepont Place. But it was a quiet understated quality, which spurned the exotic or flashy. This was all part of his commitment to the old sober ways of English Catholics. So it was rather strange when in 1835 he lured members of the Italian Institute of Rosminians to play a central role in the development of the college's spiritual life. The leader of the group, which came to Prior Park, was the renowned Fr Gentili. He had a reputation for being a powerful preacher and was responsible for the conversion of many to the Catholic Church. But wise heads were shaken. 'It would never work!' they said. Certainly

The Priory was built with stones from the Benedictine Grange at the Fishponds. The building now forms part of the girls' boarding house.

Gentili approached his new task with sepulchral foreboding. In England he would be 'exposed to continual warfare' not only 'with heresy but with its effects, consisting in corruption and low degrading vice.' The British were not only a bunch of heretics but 'cold by nature.' Grimly he girded up his loins to be 'Our Lady's advocate, procurator and champion, to reclaim from the devil the rich dowry of my Queen and Mother.' His wise Superior Rosmini pleaded with him to approach his mission with a lighter heart. 'Go around with a friendly smile'

Rosmini counselled 'do not look at things that happen in England with dark spectacles. Try to make yourself gradually English.' But it was to be of no avail.

All Gentili's apprehensions seemed confirmed when he landed in London on a dark gloomy day. This was 'the City of Pluto' he declared –'black houses, black sky – here Evil is enthroned!' And when he reached Prior Park things seemed no better – 'No one speaks of ceremonies' he complained,' there is little mention of Our Lady and never a rosary.' But Gentili was nothing if he was not a fighter. With his two assistants Anthony Rey and Emilius Belisy, he set out to lick Prior Park into proper Roman shape. By the following year Passion Week was observed as a full retreat for the College in total silence. Such austerities were soon to afflict the rest of school life. Sunday was said to have been observed with 'Trappist severity'. Pupils would rise at 6am; there would be Prayers and Mass at 6.30am followed by pious reading and meditation in the round study without a fire. Later in the morning there was High Mass and in the afternoon Vespers. The day of rest was rounded off from 5pm –7pm with 'the terrors of catechism severely administered.' No wonder Mr Kavanagh shook his head and declared that this was a regime for monks not for boys. Indeed there is clear evidence that austerity, combined with excessive devotion and rigid discipline, imposed great strain. Parents began to complain and in 1837 there was a significant decline in the number of pupils. On the Sunday before the summer vacation in 1840 there broke out in St Peter's, what Guibara calls, 'an epidemic of madness.' Returning from Vespers, some of the older pupils broke into the 'cassock room' and proceeded, 'amidst wildest jubilation' to vandalise the cassocks. Too much religion, it has been said, can make you go off pop! The savagery of Fr Hutton's response, with its brutal caning and whipping, led to an outburst of parental protest. Hutton was removed from his post and the wise Old Jem acquired more power and influence.

Baines had been very supportive of Fr Gentili's leadership. 'Very learned – very holy', he had called him. In fact the bishop had placed, against Rosmini's advice, more confidence in this charismatic priest than he should have done. Lady Mary Arundel had been so delighted by the Rosminians' development of the College's worship that she had taken up residence in the Mansion. But the Lady Mary was no fool. Right from the start she predicted that it would prove 'quite impossible for the Rosminians and Baines to go together.' Indeed Baines was already stirring uneasily at the introduction of what he considered to be new fangled Italian religious practices. When a fairly harmless statue appeared, he cried, 'Let us have no 'Romanising' here. Take it away!' Devotions to the Sacred Heart and the Immaculate Conception, he held to be simply 'inopportune'. When parents complained about the appearance of medals and scapulars, Baines took their side in opposing such un-British ways. It has to be said that, as with his own order, he seems to have shown scant understanding of the religious way of life. The daily hour's meditation, which was, not surprisingly, part of the Rosminian routine was dismissed by Baines as 'a waste of time'. Mutual irritation turned into a fatal explosion when some of the secular priests at Prior Park wanted to become Rosminians. That, the bishop realised, would take them out of his control. He for his part had already begun to try to use the Rosminian priests in the Catholic mission outside Prior Park. The arrangement was to unravel over the issue, which was always central in dealings with Baines, that of 'control'. In 1842 the inevitable happened and the Rosminians withdrew from Prior Park.

5

THE PHOENIX AFIRE

It was during the Rosminian time, in 1836, that there was the first great Prior Park fire. On 30 May at 3 pm a small boy George Manley spotted smoke coming from the Mansion roof. The dutiful child reported this to a prefect who took no notice. No doubt little boys always imagined such things or were up to such tricks! However, by 5 pm even sceptical prefects could not ignore the fact that the Mansion was indeed on fire. In no time it was all hands to the buckets. Boys were rescuing books from the Library, Henry Field was dismantling his precious organ, while the scholarly Fr Antonio Rey was only just saved from plunging into the furnace as he cried, 'Oh my Treatise De Ecclesia! Let me get it!' By the time firemen had arrived with their engines a vast crowd had begun to gather. It was said to have eventually numbered some 10 to 11 thousand. An eye-witness describes, 'the mob ranged on the hill behind the Mansion, as though in the tiers of an amphitheatre; where with eager and countless faces they scanned for hours the fearful conflagration which was raging below.' Great cheers went up every time someone emerged from the building with a rescued item. Commendation

The fire of 1836 from a picture at Prior Park.

Right: *The Hunstrete fireplace in the Library.*

Below: *Detail of the plasterwork above the Library fireplace.*

Above: *One of the Hunstrete plasterwork panels which form part of the ceiling in the Academy Hall. These were painstakingly reproduced after the fire of 1991.*

Left: *Part of the Library ceiling.*

was paid for crowd control to the Peelers, the new police force which was said to have made its first public appearance in Bath at this memorable fire.

The loss sustained by this disaster was estimated to be £15,000. As is so often the case, insurance covered only part of this – just £5500. But while a visitor mourned 'this scene of desolation and destruction', it took more than a fire to destroy Baines's dream. At once the indefatigable bishop set to work to restore the mansion 'grander and more beautiful than ever it had been.' Not far from Bath Hunstrete House had also suffered from fire and was now being demolished. Baines, prowling around the ruins, espied and coveted good things for the rebuilding of Prior Park. He bought up a staircase, oak panelling, ceilings and fire-places, which were to become such splendid features of the restored mansion. For the exterior he acquired four pagan statues. These, by means of a bit of cement and plaster, were converted into Popes and Saints. Exposure to the weather was swiftly to strip them of this veneer of sanctity and return them to their original pagan state providing surely a gift to subsequent preachers anxious to impress upon pupils the corrosive effects of 'the world, the flesh and the devil'. The restoration was completed remarkably quickly, leaving Mgr Shepherd amazed as 'the Mansion, Phoenix-like, arose speedily from the ashes, grander and more beautiful than ever it had been.'

The Academy Hall which contains much of the Hunstrete plasterwork. One of today's uses for the room is for those sitting their A level examinations.

But the true cost was still to be counted. Brindle, who had now left Pierrepont Place and joined his old friend at the College, was the Bursar. It was in truth not a great appointment. Even before the fire he was said to be sorely behind hand in paying the bills. A worried Fr Burgess wrote 'The Bishop is incomprehensible on the subject of expenses. He trusts to Providence in a way that seems to me rash-ness.' With unbounded optimism Baines launched an appeal in 1836 even request-ing 'the Protestant citizens of Bath' to contribute. That earned the not totally unfair response from the Rector of St Michael's that, although 'the Roman Trojan Horse' was 'wide enough to admit our gold', it was 'so narrow as to exclude our souls.' But although the appeal never reached its target, Baines was undeterred. Colleagues noticed that he seemed to get something of a buzz when he was 'up to his ears in mortar.' By now he was dreaming of a great new basilica, the plans of which show that its dome would have towered some 80–100 feet over the Mansion, and of the possibility of the College expanding beyond school and seminary to become a great Catholic university.

As Baines soared higher into fantasy he also plunged deeper into financial troubles and found that old problems would not go away. He was quarrelling again with his fellow Benedictines – this time over the control of the Pierrepont Place Chapel. Who was in charge, Bishop or Monastery? Nor had the depredations of Ampleforth been forgotten. What about that portrait of St Ambrose and where was compensation for those cows? In 1840 came new troubles. The 'high' Anglican Oxford Movement was leading a number of Anglicans to become Roman Catholics. Fervent converts fanned out through the Continent and there discovered all sorts of devotional delights which were not to be found in England and they returned home as missionaries for a richer more colourful spirituality. Their zeal was greater than their wisdom. That foremost of Anglican converts, John Henry Newman, was troubled by this proud and aggressive spirit and Baines's old Catholic heart again shrank from the sort of excesses that seemed to exaggerate the very things which divided Christians. He penned a fiery Pastoral Letter condemning such 'indiscrete novelties' and tried to damp down the growing spirit of triumphalism by forbidding in his district public prayer at weekday masses for the conversion of England. That stirred up a new enmity from the increasingly fashionable 'ultramontanes' who like their many successors were quick to fire off complaints to Rome. There in the Vatican the file marked 'Baines' was now positively bulging. In May 1840 the bishop was summoned to Rome to face, amongst other things, the charge of 'flattering Protestants.' In the end the Pope was to rule that Baines had exhibited no clear error, but by letter rebuked him and sent him away somewhat humiliated.

The entrance gates and lodge.

Which is not at all how his fan club at Prior Park saw it. On 27 April 1841 their bishop was welcomed home as a conquering hero. Boys met his carriage at the gates and themselves drew him to the Mansion. At the steps a song, in praise of their 'Parent, Pastor and Guide', specially composed by Fr Rooker with music by C.W. Manners, was sung.

'He comes, and let youth with a fervent devotion
In raptures unbounded his welcome proclaim;
Let age with a deeper but calmer emotion,
With eyes beaming pleasure, repeat his dear name!'

Then, as the newly founded *Tablet* recorded, all proceeded to the John Wood Chapel to sing a Te Deum and receive a solemn pontifical blessing. The event was rounded off with fireworks.

But not even such celebrations and tokens of affection could dispel the gathering clouds. A papal rebuke and the evident anxiety of his fellow bishops over the financial situation of the College brought gloom even to the ever-ebullient Baines. His health began to be affected and in March 1842 he had a mild stroke. By the summer he seemed to be recovering sufficiently to preside in June over the Corpus Christi procession and to give Benediction of the Blessed Sacrament, from those very steps, which he had built, to the whole City of Bath. That was to prove his farewell to the place, which he had so loved. Certainly he was able to be present on 4 July at the Annual Exhibition of the boys' work and the following day to preside at the Mass for the opening of the Church of St Mary on the Quay in the centre of Bristol. At this he is reported to have preached a notable sermon. So much so that the College was said to have been fairly buzzing with excitement over their hero's success and when Baines returned in the evening to a great dinner in the Mansion, the boys lurked in the background, as for some sporting hero or pop star, just to catch a mere glimpse of him. The Bishop did not however feel well enough to join the dinner and retired to his room to take just a little chicken and a glass of wine. He then went early to bed.

'Pagan' statues outside the Mansion. Converted into Popes and Saints, the veneer of sanctity was soon washed away.

Next morning the chronicler Guibarra was serving Fr Ryan's Mass. It was to have been for Saints Peter and Paul. But, as they stood at the foot of the altar for the penitential rite, the news came that Baines had been found dead in his room. At once Fr Ryan returned to the sacristy, took off the red vestments and put on the black, and, wrote that server, 'the Mass that was to have been a joyful one of our college patrons was said instead for the repose of our founder's soul.' 'Alas! Alas!' he wrote, 'those awful words Dies Irae, Dies Illa, kept sounding all through that Mass.' Old Jem led his boys up to the Bishop's death chamber there ' to kiss the Bishop's hands and take a last look at that most beautiful face.' The emotional temperature of the occasion was heightened by a frightful thunderstorm which broke and by tales told by the housekeeper, old Mother Spence, who said she had seen 'a huge ball of fire descending from the highest heavens until it rested on the Mansion right over the Bishop's room.'

At the request of the citizens of Bath, both Catholic and Protestant, the Bishop's body lay in state in the Mansion Hall. Over two days ten thousand mourners came up the hill to pay their respects. It was said that, when finally the doors were closed, there were still some two thousand left disappointed. The funeral Mass on 13 July was a grand and solemn occasion. There remains a curious puzzle over the burial of Baines. It seems that he was given a temporary resting place, no doubt in the hope that he would be finally buried within the planned Basilica.

Bishop Baines dreamed of a grand new basilica which would tower over the Mansion.

There is a macabre story of a Downside monk wandering through the buildings after the college had closed in 1856 and just coming across four abandoned coffins lying in a dismantled chapel, one of which turned out to be that of Peter Augustine Baines. Downside, with great charity, overlooked the quarrels of the past and received their brother monk's body in to the monastery cemetery. But it was not in fact until 1909 that Baines was to find his final resting place in a very grand tomb in the Downside Abbey Church. There to this day he lies alongside his old Episcopal colleague Bishop Collingridge, a sign of reconciliation with the Benedictine community yet with a touch of quiet heaping of coals by his long suffering brethren.

6

THE PHOENIX'S FIRST DEATH

With Baines dead 'the centre of gravity was no more; the master mind had gone.' Old Jem stuck to his post but all the time shook his head over the twelve years of what he called 'shiftless, thriftless, purposeless existence.' Old Fr Brindle who had proved less than adequate as a bursar had been wisely retired. But now less wisely he was to be persuaded to re-emerge as the new President. The combination of Brindle, who was something of a recluse by nature, and the new Bishop Baggs who, although amiable, lacked the drive and commitment to the College of his predecessor, was not what the situation needed. Following in the footsteps of charismatic pioneers is never enviable. It requires a steady nerve and strong resolve neither of which Brindle and Baggs possessed. They certainly did good things for the College's musical tradition. Baggs was responsible for introducing the famed Signor Rivalli to direct the music and it was he who cut Baines's Basilica down to the size of the present chapel and indeed presided over the laying of its foundation stone. This new design was by J.J. Scoles and was based on the eighteenth-century Parisian church Saint-Philippe-du-Roule. When its foundations were laid they struck a spring and, as the water flowed, bystanders wondered whether this was a sign of new life and new hope. Old Jem was a bit more practical about it. He argued that they could utilize this 'super-abundance of water' and refresh the college's empty

Above: *The deed of gift of Bishop Baines for the lands of Prior Park which is displayed in the Mansion.*

Left: *Bishop Baines' seal and papers on display in the Bishop's Library.*

coffers by supplying water to the neighbouring parts of Bath. Old Jem shook his head once again over another opportunity not seized.

Although Dr Brindle was a great favourite of the old Bishop, he was soon judged to be 'hopelessly unequal to the work' at the helm. That it could be said of any head of a school as was said of Brindle that 'he never attempted the work of teaching or superintendence' seems fairly decisively to count against his suitability for the job. Certainly he lived the life of a gentleman 'keeping a sort of state in the central mansion which was truly palatial.' The quiet routine of his daily life must be the envy of all his successors. It was his custom to rise and say the early Mass and then, having broken his fast, would write some letters. After which he would walk down the hill in a leisurely fashion to the city where he would go either to the Reading Room or to visit a few friends. He would return in the afternoon to Prior Park where, at an early hour, he would dine, normally by himself, but always in some style 'with a certain display of plate'. Such was a day in the life of Dr Brindle. 'Poor Brindle is out of his element', wrote Fr Burgess. The financial situation was certainly galloping out of control. The College was further plunged into debt by his insistence on driving ahead with the building of the new Chapel. It hardly spread sweetness and light around Bath as the mutterings grew that Brindle was 'much behind hand in the payment of his bills'. Things got so bad that Charles Fisher, Baines's old servant, was dispatched down town to pawn the College plate. That may have reduced the style of Brindle's dining but it did meet the most urgent needs – for the time being.

The Chapel in 1870, before the roof was added.

It was soon sensed that the ship was sinking. Both staff and pupils began to drift away. James Kavanagh remained loyally at his post but often sadly bewailing the drift to disaster. 'There was no head, no system' he complained 'There was stinginess where there should have been hospitality, and extravagance where there should have been economy.' At one stage the staff was reduced to Brindle, Kavanagh, and George Shepherd. It is a signal token of that old boy Guibara's affection for the college that he abandoned a promising business career in the north of England to come back to teach in this hour of need. He had no regrets for he admitted that he was captivated by the place and rejoiced that he had gained a 'paradise' in exchange for black Manchester and Glasgow. Old Jem ensured that as the ship sank, it went down gracefully 'with the consolation of good fellowship.' Of an evening they would read the poetry of Byron to one another or talk over their wine about Horace. One day Old Jem would be organising an excursion to the Bratton races where he insisted that they mingle 'with the riff-raff' and the next enticing his colleagues into a 'night of supreme enjoyment' at the Theatre Royal watching some low brow farce 'Slasher and Crasher.' Meanwhile the dwindling number of boys in the years 1854-55 enjoyed a last minute flourishing of the college's music and drama.

In the end the College's fate was sealed by a new bishop. Poor amiable Bishop Baggs had only lasted two years. Now Prior Park had cause to tremble for in his place was appointed Ullathorne, a monk from the enemy camp at Downside. As it turned out, what the College had to fear was not some mean-spirited settling of old scores, but the blunt plain-speaking new Bishop's ability to face facts. Here was a big man, a man of action, who had seen Episcopal service in the tough school of Australia where he had exercised a truly impressive ministry amongst the most deprived and often the most depraved. With a track record like this he was not likely to take kindly to what he called the 'genteel inability of Dr Brindle.' But like many another coming from those parts, he underestimated the old doctor's ability to meet his fiery bowling with a gentlemanly dead bat. For a while these two clearly incompatible characters had to share the Mansion and Brindle made it as uncomfortable for the bishop as he could. Ullathorne found that he could only communicate with the President by formal written messages carried to and fro by Brindle's valet. Eventually the Bishop was driven from Prior Park by this coldness and, with some relief, took up residence in King's Square, Bristol. But on leaving he asked for papers and records of his predecessor to take with him. The answer came that there were none. In fact the affairs of the Western District and the College had become so muddled that they could not be disentangled.

The 1996 Chapel organ.

Ullathorne was to give a long description of his dealings with Prior Park. It is clear that he shared the Rosminian view of its religion, not only judging Brindle to be a rather worldly man, but everything there to be 'stamped all over, inside and out, with a secular tone.' There were no statues of the saints and only one visible cross. All in all a very 'minimising' spirit prevailed. It was probably through Ullathorne that a dark story went the rounds. Some priest opening up a deserted looking tabernacle in the college found to his horror a Host withered and black-ened with age. It is a tale to be sniffed at with some suspicion, for it hardly accords with what we know of the rather fastidious care, which Baines had always taken of sacred buildings and their contents. He may not have encouraged what he regarded as 'flashy' innovations but he did promote decency and reverence. So it has to be said that this story bears all the marks of priestly gossip and hostile prop-aganda. Moreover, set against Ullathorne's strictures, are the reflections of John

Henry Newman. He visited Prior Park in 1845 and liked what he saw. Yes, it was a rather 'worldly set out' but that to him seemed somewhat refreshing after the wild enthusiasms and sickly piety of his fellow converts. 'Dr Brindle' he wrote 'is a gentleman in the true sense of the word.' This might not be a 'school of perfection' but it was a place of 'sensible as well as earnest religion.' If it's whole 'set-out is gentlemanlike' it also had 'the deep impression of religion.' How could it be otherwise with the Blessed Sacrament in it? Indeed Newman rather warmed to the way of life at Prior Park. It reminded him of the old days in an Oxford college. The judgement of the Abbot of St Bernard's Monastery was positively effusive. He found in the College 'a piety, a regularity, a recollection, a zeal for the honour of God and the advancement of the Catholic faith' which 'ravished his heart with excessive joy.'

But not even such ravishing piety could pay the bills. Brindle continued to be uncooperative with his Bishop. So it is not surprising that, in the end, Ullathorne had to pass the matter to Rome with the request that there be set up a commission of enquiry into the affairs of Prior Park. This was done and the greatly respected Bishop Griffiths presided over it. He was swift to rebuke Brindle for his resistance to his Bishop. 'As your Bishop gradually and justly grows displeased with you' he wrote 'you show no sense of it and his words are like balls fired at a woolsack, they drop dead and without effect, from your passive resistance to his voice.' Even Brindle's best friends knew that he must go. At this decisive stage there was yet another Episcopal change. Ullathorne was translated to the Central District where, after the formal introduction of the Hierarchy and the re-establishment of Catholic dioceses in 1850, he became the first Archbishop of Birmingham. Bishop Hendren came to the Western District and was shortly to become the first Bishop of Clifton. So it fell to him to implement the conclusions of the commission. Accordingly he proposed the removal of Brindle from the Presidency of the College. The old doctor showed that he would not go willingly, refusing to quit unless he were repaid the £8000 he had himself ploughed into the enterprise. Yet on 30 October 1849 Brindle had to face the inevitable. He was finally ousted and was replaced by his old friend and colleague 'Daddy' Rooker. It was said though, that when he saw that the game was up, Brindle acted 'admirably – not a word of objection, nor any complaint, not a look of unkindness'.

The Most Reverend George Errington DD, Archbishop of Trebizond.

But even this drastic action could not solve the financial crisis. Despite a visit by Rooker to Rome to plead for the saving of the College, Bishop Hendren made it clear that he felt no obligation to preserve the College at all costs. A respite was provided from an unexpected source, Alexander Raphael the MP for St Albans, who was himself a Catholic. He purchased Prior Park and then leased it to the College Trustees for a very modest rent. But not even this act of generosity could delay the inevitable. Bishop Hendren was whisked off to become the new Bishop of Nottingham, and Rome rather ominously decided that no new bishop of Clifton would be appointed until the affairs of Prior Park could be sorted out. Such were the affairs of Diocese and College intermingled! The Co-Adjutor Archbishop of

Above: *The Errington Chapel.*

Right: *The Errington Corridor as it is today.*

Westminster Dr Errington was appointed administrator of the Diocese with a particular brief to bring this long-running saga to a conclusion. This he did with admirable speed. Although Errington was to become the most loyal of friends of Prior Park both teaching there and indeed ending his days there he saw that now its affairs were simply hopeless. At this point the admirable Alexander Raphael, who had been paid not a penny of his rent, decided to take possession of the buildings. This was the signal for the College's many creditors to swoop on its goods and chattels. They proposed that everything should be sold off by public auction. After such a glorious start came now the humiliation of six days during which its bits and bobs were exhibited to the public gaze. Bishop Errington who had faced up to the inevitable could hardly bear it. It was, he said, 'lamentable and vexing to hear the comments and see the profanity of heretics at the show.' The auction began on 21 February 1856 and lasted for all of sixteen days. The total realised by the sale, £6382, proved just enough to meet the outstanding debts.

As everything was disintegrating around them a remnant of staff continued to serve a remnant of pupils. The President, old 'Daddy' Rooker, by now having to live with friends down in Bath daily 'toiled and stumped up that interminable hill' to teach the three or four remaining boys. When he at last reached the College he was to be seen 'sitting down and placidly wiping his bald head, and looking dejectedly over his spectacles at the boys.' All the while the broker's men were moving amongst them slapping tickets on the benches they sat on or cataloguing the class books they held in their hands. Old Jem also stayed to the bitter end. Guibara describes his friend's last melancholy hours at the College. He went round to all the old spots that were so endeared to him through memories of his boys – the ball-place, the football field, the long class room, the Bishop's Chapel, all the old haunts near the Rainbow Wood and by the ponds. 'He gave one fond lingering look from the portico and then the brave old man bade his last good bye to the home of so many friendships and so many recollections, and with a broken heart went down the "Mons Sacer" which he was never again to see save in his dreams.'

THE RISE OF THE PHOENIX – THE DR WILLIAMS ERA

Now what was to be done with Ralph Allen's Mansion? Mr Raphael did not want to live in it and was indeed quite keen to get it off his hands. There were some nuns in Taunton who for a while seemed quite attracted by it, but nothing came of that. Government inspectors considered it for a barracks and the awful rumour went round that Louis Napoleon was poised to take it over as a place to teach French officers English. Old critics of the College rather fancied the suggestion that it might be turned into a 'madhouse'. But, as it turned out, there was to be life still in the dream of Peter Augustine Baines. After running through a remarkable number of bishops and seeming to have reached a final resolution of the Prior Park Problem, there was now appointed to the Diocese of Clifton a great friend of the College, William Joseph Hugh Clifford, the Vicar General in Plymouth. Here was a man who stood in the old Baines tradition of English Catholicism, one who, when the heady brew of ultramontanism with its papal extremism and Vatican centralism went to the heads of the episcopate, remained calm and critical. At the First Vatican Council he was with the minority of those who, like Newman, held a decree on papal infallibility to be 'inopportune'. When Clifford died the affection in which he was held was made clear. They spoke at his funeral of 'an honest man, a good man, a God fearing man, a kind man, an able man and one who deserved to be called a lover of his brethren.' Like Baines he wanted Catholics to be a bit less angular and more willing to be lovers of and workers for the common good of society. He himself delighted to be a gospel seed falling into the ground of this West Country corner of the vineyard. He was deeply interested in its history and something of an amateur archaeologist. On such matters he was to read many a learned paper to the Bath Literary and Scientific Society. But what matters above all for this story, was that he had been a student at Prior Park and now openly mourned its demise.

The Right Reverend William Joseph Clifford DD.

The new Bishop saw it as a matter of urgency that the educational gap left by the College should be filled. So he set up in Clifton the Bristol Catholic Grammar School. Many openly considered this to be just 'Prior Park in exile'. As head of this school Clifford appointed the thirty-six-year-old priest who served Catholics in Frome and Chippenham, Dr Williams, who, as another old boy of Prior Park, shared his Bishop's love and enthusiasm for the old place. Soon the two of them were not only dreaming but also actively plotting to end the College's exile in Bristol. The very prospect of such a revival many friends thought to be total madness. Old Lord Clifford, the bishop's father, declared that it was 'a white elephant' and Fr Fred Neve that the 'place had a curse on it.' Yet the moment seemed opportune, for Prior Park was on the market again. The Bishop took to the Cathedral Chapter the proposal that the Diocese should buy it back and the Canons agreed that the College in exile should return to its proper home.

Cricket's manly toil.

With 'breaking voice and hands trembling – with ill concealed excitement' Dr Williams addressed his pupils in Clifton. 'Boys!' he declared 'I have been sent to acquaint you with an important decision of the Chapter. Instead of yonder tiny plot of grass would you like to have a large field in which to play your games? Instead of having a long walk to the Downs to seek a pitch for your stumps or a vacant space for your football, would you like a large field within sight of the house?' And on continued the Doctor to paint an ever more alluring picture of this Promised Land ending with the thunderous declaration 'If you would like these things, then I have to tell you that they are yours, for the re-purchase of Prior Park is an accomplished fact!' This great speech was constantly interrupted with the boys' cheers and shouts of 'Yes! Yes! We would!' After all this excitement Williams sobered up a bit and from this moment, it was said, 'his face often wore a thoughtful expression, as if he were already anticipating and pondering over the difficult task entrusted to him.'

On 23 April 1867 'all was bustle, confusion and excitement' as everything in Clifton was packed up to be dispatched to Bath. Then Dr Williams and the boys went down to Temple Meads station to catch the train for Bath Spa. When they alighted the Doctor led them up the hill to their new home. A boy who had been on that route march later wrote: ' Though the walk was long and the sun shone, the Doctor kept us on the alert by continually asserting that we were at the point of reaching the College gates and that the next turning would bring us in sight of the buildings.' Others who have followed these pilgrims up that hill know only too well the ever-elusive nature of that 'last' turn. But on arrival the returning exiles were given a hearty welcome by their Promised Land.

Within a week the College was back into the swing of its studies. Assisting the Doctor in his formidable task were Canon Shattock, Fathers J. Macdonald and D. Hubert, along with Williams's own younger brother James. Unlike his predecessor Brindle, this President did his own fair share of the teaching. His language was said at all times to be 'refined and ornamental' and there was perhaps a touch of pedantry about him. He was much enamoured of philology and could not resist holding up a lesson to point out at some length the derivation of words.

Plunged into the pages of the lexicon 'he seemed lost to all his surroundings.' Of course this was spotted and exploited by the wilier members of the class who would 'indulge in a little gentle play' of guiding the Doctor into these delightful diversions. No doubt all this fascination with words and their meaning sprang from his love of the classics. With two other ecclesiastics Williams had the job of preparing the Latin text for those official gatherings of the Catholic hierarchy in Britain, called the Provincial Synods. On one occasion Dr Williams found fault with the use of the indicative mood when there should have been the subjunctive. The discussion of this matter took two meetings of the translating committee and was only resolved when the Doctor triumphantly appeared with a volume of Cicero which proved his contention. His love of the classics led him to aspire to see the College produce a Greek play but alas the result was less than encouraging. But Williams, unlike many contemporary schoolmasters, was not imprisoned by the classics. He was a good all-round linguist, speaking both French and Italian, and able at least to read German. Following his morning ablutions, in a short gap before going to the Chapel to say Mass, he would spend a few minutes wrestling with Italian irregular verbs. It is not surprising therefore that Williams encouraged the teaching of modern languages in the College.

The revived Phoenix swiftly rose. Numbers grew and the returned exiles who had started by simply occupying the St Paul's building had now to expand into St Peter's. The heart of Baines would have warmed by the fact that in 1870 the Mansion was opened up for senior theological students thus fulfilling again the College's role as a seminary to train priests for the diocese. All these developments meant that President Williams could himself teach less and had to organize more. Yet he always remained essentially a pastoral leader. His undemonstrative exterior hid, they said, a warm heart. He cared for his pupils as individuals. He loved to accompany them on long walks or take them on excursions to the city, especially to its Roman baths.

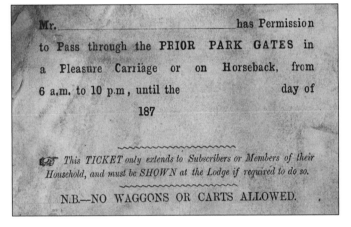

Ticket to visit the grounds and admire the buildings and views of Bath.

If a boy were seriously ill, it would be the President who insisted on sitting with him through the night 'speaking words of encouragement, consolation and hope.' The one thing he really hated as head of a school was having to expel a boy. 'You will never know' he said, 'unless by actual experience, how terrible is the duty of having to inform a father or mother that their boy is being sent home.'

Yet with success the College's finances remained fragile. 'Many anxious and sleepless hours of night were spent devising ways and means of dealing with an ever increasing expenditure.' Friends said that it was 'a mystery how amidst the worries and trials of his position he always preserved so unruffled and calm an exterior.' The secret lay in his solid unostentatious God-centred piety – at the foot of the altar and in those frequent visits to his Lord in the Blessed Sacrament. Williams's religion was deep and real without being narrow or sectarian. In fact he hated the sectarian spirit, loathed all bigotry or any trace of the persecuting spirit. Rather than being quick to criticise others with whom he disagreed he was eager 'to ascribe honesty of purpose to all'. He even managed to cultivate good relations with Downside! When a fellow Catholic reacted with understandable belligerence to a particularly nasty Protestant taunt, Williams deliberately and gracefully 'turned the conversation from the paths of aggression.' Better to cool it than to strike back.

Seymour Hicks performing in 1884.

Sir Seymour Hicks.

Like his Bishop Clifford, he delighted to immerse himself in the life of Bath, again also delivering to the Literary and Philosophical Association 'polished and scholarly papers.' His love of music also led him down into the city to enjoy, what were called, 'high-class concerts' and, back in the College, he energetically encouraged the development of its musical life. On the Feast of St Cecilia, the patron saint of music, there would each year be a concert over which the Doctor himself presided with great care. He was said to be 'one of the few teachers who can obtain the full volume of voice in a choir of boys without suffering them to shout.' With growing conviction Williams came to recognise that 'music and drama was by no means a frivolous element in a boy's education.' A famous Prior Park old boy, the actor Seymour Hicks, later paid warm tribute to these enlightened views. At a time when many considered the calling of an actor to be one 'fit only for rogues and vagabonds' the old Doctor positively encouraged him in the pursuit of this career. Its foundations were laid not only in Hicks singing solo 'O Salutaris' at the opening of the new chapel but also, at the age of nine, in his appearance as Buttercup in Gilbert and Sullivan's HMS *Pinafore*. The later knighted Sir Seymour Hicks expressed his gratitude for what he called the 'broadmindedness' of Prior Park under Dr Williams and paints an attractive picture of the President 'smiling with kindly eyes through gold-rimmed spectacles upon his little kingdom.' Hicks was not the only one to discover his theatrical vocation at Prior Park, Maurice Noel from Devon was another. He wrote farces for the theatre, one of which reached the Criterion in the West End and was said by *Punch* to be 'stronger than milk and water and a very refreshing tonic after a hard day's work.'

The Prior Park Association v College Cricket Teams of 1884.

Williams's enthusiasm spread to the sports field. He was himself an accomplished footballer and something of an athlete. It was rumoured that he was able to jump the width of the canal. This was the time when golf was beginning to catch on and Williams played a leading part in the development of the game in Bath. He himself won 'a liberal share of prizes' and was said to have revealed his piety when, like all other golfers ' he failed an easy stroke,' responded 'without seeking consolation in golfers' usual pet ejaculations.' On his deathbed he remembered in prayer his many golfing friends and later, at his funeral, Bath golfers, both male and female, were present. For some years, a photo of the old Doctor hung in the Sham Castle Club house.

But it was cricket which was his greatest love and which had most influence on the life of the College. Williams himself had developed as a useful bowler and a careful bat. Every year on the cricket field at Claverton he delighted to have something of a personal duel with his good friend the solicitor Mr Frank King. All this devotion to the game inspired the College to some truly golden years of cricketing. Every success was celebrated in style. In the grounds the Doctor had an old cannon, which he fired on the occasion of every 1st XI victory, and, in that late nineteenth-century period, there must have been a lot of cannon fire. On 5 May 1887 the College defeated Downside by an innings and 62 runs and that is but one of a truly impressive list of triumphs, which included decisive victories over the Gloucester Nondescripts, the Horfield Garrison and Lansdown. Such was the boys' zeal for the game that the season was decreed to begin after Easter Day irrespective of whether the feast came late or early. One year in Easter week and 'under dull leaden skies with a cold wind', W. Harold Barry scored 200 runs in one innings. It was said of him at his death that 'his life had been a really good innings and he had always played with a straight bat'! H. Bilsborrow excelled as 'an energetic and hard working captain' and W. Bisgood who launched his cricketing career at the College found it to be a long one for, as a parish priest in the

Maintenance of the cricket pitch has always been vital. Messrs Fox, Rimmer, O'Neil, Beresford and de Freitas are among those hard at work.

A photograph taken on the Mansion steps in the Dr Williams era.

Cotswolds, he was still keeping wicket in his sixties. The cricket enthusiasm of the President was matched by that of Bishop Clifford who believed strongly in 'cricket's manly toil' and put his money where his mouth was with generous financial contributions towards the improvement of the cricket field.

Reading through the school magazines of this period one catches something of a late nineteenth century imperial glow. The records are full of news of old boys like Captain James Hennessy writing on the 'natives' of New Guinea or Captain Chichester going off to Hyderabad for the Pig-Sticking but only managing to 'bag a few partridge and quail'. There is a detailed article in the 1892 magazine on the hardships of life on a troopship bound for Bombay. A thousand men are crammed together living on 'tinned boiled mutton alternating with salt beef and salt pork' – all unalleviated by supplies of either tobacco or alcohol. However, on arriving at Poona and enjoying a day at the races the writer concludes that 'soldiering will be an easy job' waited on as they were by those 'natives' who seemed to him 'very picturesque rascals'!

While Prior Park dispatched its emissaries to the furthest corners of Empire, at home the College celebrated in 1887 Queen Victoria's Jubilee. On Sunday 19 June, High Mass was sung 'in thanksgiving for the blessings conferred on the country during the Queen's reign.' The service concluded with a 'Te Deum' and a 'Domine Salvam fac Reginam' arranged especially for the occasion by Mns. Nourry, and, as the procession moved towards the sacristy, Mr A. Williams played the National Anthem on the organ. The following Tuesday celebrations continued in a more secular vein. The school magazine describes in loving detail how a bonfire was prepared for the occasion. It sounds like every Health and Safety Inspector's nightmare, involving not only 'dry faggots and brushwood – loose straw and shavings' but also 'twelve gallons of petroleum.' There was added to this a full barrel of tar. It was thought to be advisable at the last minute to shoot a bullet into this barrel to let some of the tar drip out over the pile 'and also to avoid the danger of its bursting.' This almost led to the demise of one of the College servants, a Mr Harris, who got deluged with tar and only just escaped the final conflagration to become a burnt offering made to Her Majesty. This awesome mass was ignited at 10pm in response to a signal passed on from the Malvern Hills. As a rocket burst 'a taper was applied to the bonfire, and in a few seconds the whole mass was enveloped in a sheet of flame, which rushed up to a height of 70 feet from the ground. Those who were present will not easily forget the fury with which the fire

A Corpus Christi procession passing St Paul's.

devoured its prey. It roared and crackled with a savage worrying sound, and threw out so fierce a heat that the circle of onlookers was drawn at a very respectful distance.' It was reported that 'the National Anthem was very well sung by the boys at the beginning and end of the proceedings.' Some bright lad had the wit to exploit the occasion of the Queen's Jubilee by writing to the Monarch herself requesting that some holiday for her young loyal subjects be granted by Royal Decree. Her famous secretary Sir Henry Ponsonby duly replied that Her Majesty bestowed upon the College an extra week's holiday.

Such were the secular jollifications but what about the College's continued witness to that Catholic faith which had given it birth? This was a bonfire which burned less fiercely than the intense piety of the Rosminians or even than the Irish piety of the later Christian Brothers. It might well have earned the Ullathorne rebuke of seeming 'rather secular' but this again would be to underestimate that quiet English Catholic style beloved of its founding father. It could be said that the Williams-Clifford era most fully expressed that ethos which Baines had sought. Now of course the Bishop of the Diocese came home where Baines always believed he belonged, in the bosom of his College. There he was able personally to oversee the work, which began again on the Scoles-designed Chapel that had for so long remained unfinished, without roof, desolate and deserted. There are photos of these wilderness years – with the Chapel open to the skies sprouting bushes and all manner of vegetation amidst which ladies with parasols can be seen wandering through its wastes. But now the work on the Chapel was completed and on 6 July 1882 its solemn opening was celebrated on the day of Bishop Clifford's own Silver Jubilee. Care was taken not only in completing this lovely building but also in what took place inside it. The College enjoyed another flourishing of liturgical music. Never, it was said, had the Holy Week services been so splendid, 'never before have the psalms been chanted with such "go"'. The Passion gospel was sung on both Palm Sunday and Good Friday, while the harmonized Lamentations drew particular praise.

Countess Isabella English.
Reproduced by kind permission
of the *Bath Chronicle*.

The College seemed to be looking to the future with some confidence. In November 1887 it was announced that 'we shall be able shortly to communicate with Bath by Telephone. The poles are already erected and it only remains for the wires to be attached.' All this was looked forward to as 'a great convenience.' Yet all such advances, in truth, rested on precarious economic foundations, and a series of deaths was to shake them. First to go in 1886 was loyal old Archbishop Errington who, disappointed of his hope of becoming Archbishop of Westminster, ended up teaching at Prior Park. He was to be followed two years later by the Countess English who had proved a most generous benefactor of the College. Then in 1891 Dr Williams himself died.

'He persevered, until the doubting stranger,
Who whispered 'Failure' could not but confess
That Prior Park in spite of storm and danger
Had budded, bloomed and blossomed to success.'

A whole edition of the *Prior Park Magazine* is given over to Williams's death. There is a long and lugubrious article signed 'a Grateful Pupil' on the 'Last Illness, Death and Funeral of the Right Rev. Monsignor Canon Williams DD'. On 2 March he had celebrated quietly his sixtieth birthday and the following day had gone off to play golf. Maybe these sporting exertions proved too much as he was seized that night with 'excruciating pains'. As his end drew near he was to send messages of love and blessing to 'the dear boys and masters'. Surrounded by six

Dr Edward Williams.

priests Williams received the last sacraments and, hand laid upon the gospels, made his final act of faith. On his death the College swung into several days of mourning. Old pupils began to gather although the winter weather was such and with 'trains snowed up for days and roads rendered impassable through snow-drifts', many more who wanted to come failed to do so. As the body lay in state in the Mansion, it was noticed that 'the boys were moving familiarly round the coffin, arranging the wreaths and crosses' showing 'that they feared him not in death, being drawn to him even then as in life by his gentleness and amiability.' At his funeral Bishop Clifford his old friend and architect, with him, of the revival of Prior Park, preached a long and moving homily. After the Mass the body was carried to its grave in what is now known as the Errington Corridor and, as the choir sang the antiphon 'Ego sum resurrectio', the body was lowered into its last resting place.

Those Williams years had indeed had been sunny years of happiness and success. Now the leadership was to pass from the charismatic Doctor to his agreeable but less colourful brother James. He simply could not generate the steam to bring the ship on through 'storm and danger'. The final blow was to be the death of Bishop Clifford in 1893. If the charisma had fled with the old Doctor, active episcopal support backed with money fled with this great architect and patron of the return. Once again the frailty of the College's economic foundations were laid bare and once again Prior Park was to become the Bishop's nightmare.

St Peter's house in the Christian Brothers' era.

8

THE FIRST CHRISTIAN BROTHER ERA

William Robert Brownlow was appointed Bishop of Clifton in 1894. He, like Clifford, had been a Vicar General of Plymouth. Once he had been an Anglican priest and had been received into the Catholic Church by John Henry Newman. Of Brownlow it was said that 'outwardly he might seem somewhat lethargic but really he had clear purposes and worked unceasingly.' Such qualities he displayed when within a year he discovered that in Prior Park he had been handed something of a poisoned chalice. Like his predecessors he found the question 'What to do with Prior Park?' came to haunt his waking and sleeping hours. But Brownlow did not sit around wringing his hands; he soon worked out a clear purpose and proceeded to act with resolution. He began to look for some religious order to take the College off his hands and this led him to write to the Superior of the Irish Christian Brothers in Limerick. Here was a new order dedicated to teaching boys, which was already making an impact and acquiring a good reputation in Ireland. The Brothers' real expertise lay with what would have deemed to have been a rather 'lower' social ranking than that to which Prior Park had been accustomed. It became their main task to educate and build up an Irish middle class. But this was no problem for Brownlow. He reckoned that the College was aiming too high that 'as a school for young gentlemen, the numbers were too small' so that 'the enterprise would always be too precarious.' However he did see the need for 'a good catholic commercial school' possibly with a 'technical school' as well.

Brother Maxwell, the Superior General of the Brothers, seemed attracted by the idea. Brownlow suggested a twenty-one-year lease on the building. Some haggling between the Brothers and the Prior Park Trustees over the rent followed this. It became quite clear at this stage that the latter were nothing like so enthusiastic about the project as their Bishop. They still wanted to keep alive Baines's dream of a Diocesan College. They sniffed suspiciously at these Irish Brothers and wondered whether great Catholic families like the Cliffords would any longer send their boys to a Prior Park run by them. However, realism seemed to be on the side of the Bishop and the negotiations were driven forward. It was at this point that a fatal ambiguity was to creep in. The Trustees made the helpful-sounding suggestion that there be a 'fair trial' period of seven years which would 'enable

William Robert Brownlow, Bishop of Clifton.

A photograph taken in about 1900 which includes Raymund Upham. St Peter's can be seen in the background.

you (i.e. the Brothers) to terminate the lease before the expiration of the twenty-one years' if things simply proved to be impossible. The attraction of this was as a let-out clause for the Congregation. As a bit of extra enticement Bishop Brownlow said that there was a need for a day school in Bristol and would the Brothers be interested in that as well?

All of which led to the next stage in the life of Prior Park College. On 17 July 1895 Br Swan came as the first Christian Brother President. By this time the school had dwindled to something of a remnant. The Brothers inherited just 55 pupils, but by the turn of the century this had grown to 110. The College Prospectus for this era advertises the beauty both of the buildings and the thirty acres of what it calls 'the Park and Pleasure Grounds'. Some measure of comfort is offered by a hot water system of heating and a Lavatory 'of the newest and most perfect kind, with bath-room annexed' and a supply of both hot and cold water. Of course, comforts of a more intellectual and spiritual kind were advertised. 'While the intellectual culture of the Students is carefully attended to, the Christian Brothers consider it their chief duty to impart a religious and moral training to those committed to their care.' The College was still divided between St Peter's for the younger ones where a Matron 'looks after the health and cleanliness of the little Boys', and St Paul's for the 'more advanced classes' which promoted a traditional 'liberal' education but also, as a sign of an attempt to widen the scope of the College, 'a Commercial Course' which included History of British Industry and Commerce, Shorthand, Type-writing and Book-keeping. The Brothers clearly did not shrink from the pursuit of 'useful' knowledge.

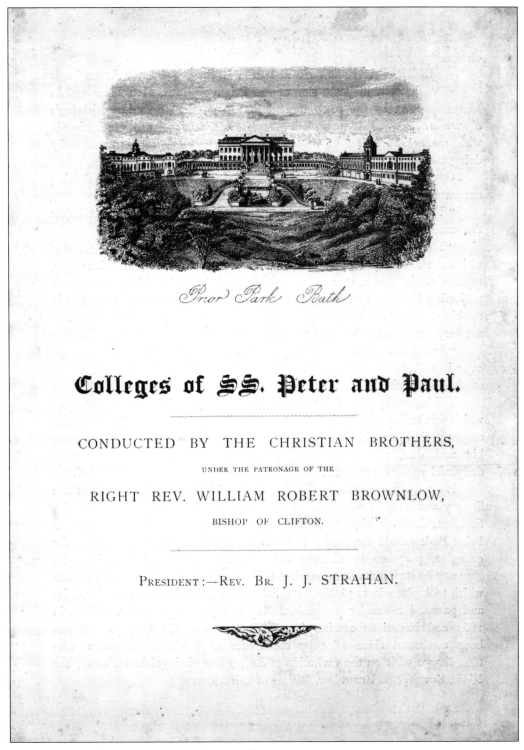

Pror Park Bath

Colleges of SS. Peter and Paul.

CONDUCTED BY THE CHRISTIAN BROTHERS,

UNDER THE PATRONAGE OF THE

RIGHT REV. WILLIAM ROBERT BROWNLOW,

BISHOP OF CLIFTON.

PRESIDENT :—REV. BR. J. J. STRAHAN.

The front page of the prospectus in the Brownlow era.

A classroom, 1900.

One of the fine new wash rooms and dormitories. This one was in St Peter's.

The Bishop's Library. Today the room is used for meetings.

The Gymnasium.

The Library in 1900. This room is now the Academy Hall, although the atrium is no longer a feature.

The Refectory which has changed very little over the years.

The Theatre, 1904. It is believed that this was in St Paul's.

An early science laboratory.

The Swimming Pool which at the time was fed by the local springs.

Roller-skating on the covered playground was a popular activity in 1900. This photograph was taken in front of what is now the Design Technology Centre. Apparently the roof of the Old Gymnasium was also allowed to flood and freeze for skating.

Under their leadership the College certainly took off again but just as the seven-year lease was coming to an end, Bishop Brownlow died. In 1902 George Ambrose Burton, the parish priest of South Shields, was appointed to succeed him. Coming from the North East he was innocent of the trials and tribulations of West Country Catholicism and therefore refreshingly free of the baggage of prejudice and partisanship, which surrounded the affairs of Prior Park. But ignorance was not entirely bliss for there were those senior powerful priests of the diocese waiting for a chance to manipulate their raw new bishop. One of the first issues to hit his desk was the ending of the seven-year lease on Prior Park. The hovering vultures saw their opportunity. The Vicar General Mgr Russell and the Prior Park Trustees moved in to argue the case that the College should return where it belonged, in the bosom of the Diocese. Now the numbers were picking up, appropriate gratitude could be expressed to the Christian Brothers for their successful rescue operation but the Baines project could be resumed. Pressure was put upon the new Bishop who was now quietly descending into what Ullathorne darkly called 'the bottomless abyss'. To further entice the Bishop in this direction the Trustees were able to dangle before his eyes the £1000 left by a member of the Eyre family for the revival of the College as such a diocesan venture. On 14 May 1902 the Trustees decided not to renew the Christian Brothers' lease.

A new Prospectus admits that for seven years the Brothers had 'carried on an excellent school' but that it was felt that 'contrary to its second founder's (i.e. Bishop Clifford's) intentions, the establishment had ceased to be a centre of diocesan interests, and accordingly one of the first cares of Bishop Burton on his accession to the See of Clifton was to bring it into close touch with the Diocese by resuming its immediate direction and control.' The Bishop, they insisted, had thereby acquired 'the jewel of the Diocese'. Soon poor Burton found it to be otherwise. From the clouds of euphoria he descended to earth as he made what must be the first telephone conversation mentioned in the school records. Rather belatedly he asked Mgr Russell – 'Who puts money into the concern?' The bland but disconcerting reply came swiftly – 'Oh you my Lord put it in!'

Prior Park notepaper used in correspondence from a member of the governing body.

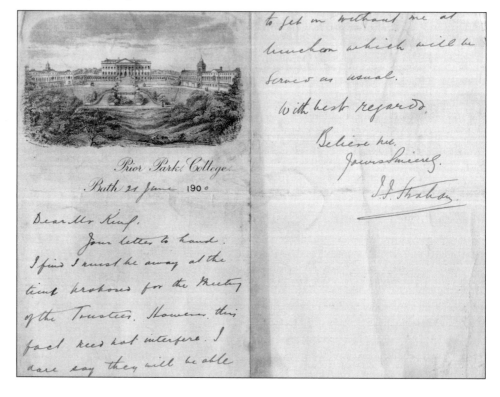

A soccer team in 1902, captained by Raymund Upham

Everyone except the Trustees reckoned that the prospects for this new stage in Prior Park's life were less than favourable. What security the Brothers had achieved for the College had been thrown away and the search for leadership in the shape of a new President proved to be difficult. Fr Horace Mann was invited down from Newcastle to view the place. He came, he saw and he pronounced it all 'a white elephant.' 'Sell it!' he counselled the Bishop. After much searching and many invitations, which were declined, finally one Edmond Nolan was appointed. He swiftly lived to regret it. When the Brothers had left, the school had 110 pupils; Nolan inherited between 20 and 30. It was not exactly a ringing parental endorsement of the new regime. However, keeping his fingers crossed and hoping for the best, at 7.30am on 16 September 1902 the Bishop said a Mass of the Holy Spirit in the new chapel and the College was up if hardly running again.

Burton was clearly uneasy about it all. He tended to keep clear of the place because, when he did visit it, he complained that he was always confronted by 'difficulties' 'difficulties with the staff, difficulties with the buildings, difficulties with the Trustees, difficulties present and difficulties future!' Not surprisingly Edmond Nolan felt less than secure in his post. The hosts of Midian began again to prowl and prowl around, particularly in the guise of that old enemy 'money' or more strictly the lack of it. The Eyre nest-egg, which had seemed so re-assuring, melted away like snow in the Current Account. Within a year Burton had to bite the bullet and in September 1903 felt it necessary himself to move into Prior Park to take control of things. By early 1904 he concluded that the College must close at the end of the school year. Getting wind of this Edmond Nolan panicked and decided to move out after Easter. Faced with the prospect of the school limping on headless for another term, the Bishop acted decisively and gathered the boys on the night before returning home for the Easter holidays to announce that in fact the school was closing there and then. On 23 April he bluntly told the Trustees that the financial situation was such that this was inevitable and irreversible. The affairs of the estate were put into the hands of the secretary to the Trustees, Mr King, the solicitor. Once again the Phoenix had wilted and died.

The staircase in St Paul's which originally continued beyond the first floor.

9

THE RETURN OF THE CHRISTIAN BROTHERS

For twenty years, from 1904 to 1924, the Phoenix lay dead; there was no Prior Park College. What then happened to Ralph Allen's mansion? For a few years it passed through several hands, including those of the Holy Ghost Fathers from Paris who leased it for three years. During the 1914-18 War, it was requisitioned by the War Office and for a while used as a Rest Home for wounded Canadian soldiers. This was to prove to be of great advantage to the College's future for, while schoolboys were thought not to need the benefits of main drainage, soldiers did, and so, at the expense of the War Office, Prior Park acquired this benefit.

Members of the 4th (RES) Battalion Prince Albert's Somerset Light Infantry on the steps of the Mansion.
Reproduced by kind permission of the Somerset Archive and Record Office.

Part of a larger photograph of 'A' Company, Officer Cadet Battalion, taken at Prior Park in the early months of 1917. Capt T.J.E. Blake, Royal Fusiliers Instructor, Lt Col W.H. Wild DSO, Battalion Commander and Capt A.E.D. Bliss (later Sir Arthur Bliss), Royal Fusiliers Instructor, are all in the front row.

After the First World War, a Cannington Industrial School, a Home Office establishment for what were then called 'maladjusted' boys, was transferred to Prior Park. This was to run into a nasty scandal. In 1919 a boy escaped and, when eventually recaptured, was treated with gross savagery. The Superintendent manacled the boy's hands behind his back and he was attached by a chain to his ankle. Showing an admirable spirit, the lad escaped again and got as far as Bath where a policeman's attention was attracted by the clanking of chains in the street. To his horror he saw that these were fixed to the blistered and bleeding limbs of a child. Instead of the escapee being quietly returned to his place of incarceration, the law proceeded against the school, the Superintendent had to resign and later, with several members of his staff, was prosecuted. The Home Office now had to ponder what was to be done with their disgraced Industrial School. At which stage it did what many others do in a fix, turned to Mother Church in its hour of need. In turn Bishop Burton handed this hot potato over to the Christian Brothers. They had shown in the past how to rescue failed enterprises, would they now please assume the management of the Industrial School?

As can be imagined the Brothers treated this invitation with some caution. They believed that they had been ill-used by the Diocese over Prior Park and no doubt shared Br Strahan's judgement that their 'moral rights' had been 'flagrantly violated' when the College had been seized back through invoking a clause in the lease in a way which was clearly not intended. What they believed had been offered as a 'let out' clause for the Brothers had, by wily clerics, been turned into an opportunity for the Diocese to snatch back their College just when they were turning things round. A bad flavour had been left in their mouths. Despite all this, however, Br Hennessy, the Superior General, eventually agreed to the Bishop's request, but only if the property were sold to the Congregation. So in 1921 the College buildings passed to the Brothers. This was just in time for the Home Office in 1924 to decide to close down its Industrial Schools. Now the Brothers had the buildings but what now was to be done with them?

Back at the end of the last century the Brothers had responded favourably to Bishop Brownlow's attempt to entice them to Bristol as well as to Bath and had set up St Brendan's College. What had started as a day school had evolved to acquire some boarding pupils. There were now 70 of these and the decision was made to transfer them to Prior Park to form the core of the new school, leaving St Brendan's as a day school. St Peter's building became again the centre for the junior school while St Paul's was to be for the seniors. This time aspirations to house also a seminary to train priests for the Diocese was dropped, but instead the Mansion became, for a while, the Novitiate home for the Christian Brothers in England.

Judgements on the years of the Christian Brothers at Prior Park can be coloured by either a crude racist suspicion of all things Irish, or the rather deplorable snobbishness of 'upper class' Catholicism in England. It was soon put around that, with the advent of the Brothers, the College had taken a nose-dive in the social pecking order. It was rumoured to be hardly the place for young gents. They should head for Downside or Ampleforth, leaving Prior Park to mop up the more intellectually challenged rugby players. Well that was not at all what the Brothers intended. As Br Forde was to put it, Prior Park was in business to produce 'educated, cultured gentlemen and intelligent practical Catholics'. Whether this was precisely the mission to which the great founder Edmund Rice had summoned his brethren may be open to question and indeed, after the Second Vatican Council when all religious orders reviewed their aims and objectives, this was to become the great issue. But for the moment the Brothers were happy to dip their toes into the growing stream of English public school life – yet, as we shall see, were never quite at ease there.

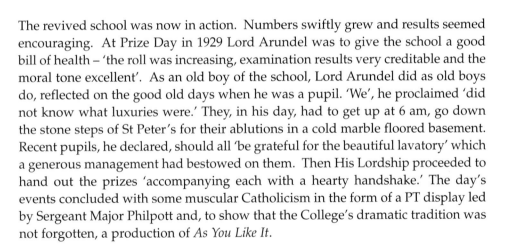

Brother Forde.

The revived school was now in action. Numbers swiftly grew and results seemed encouraging. At Prize Day in 1929 Lord Arundel was to give the school a good bill of health – 'the roll was increasing, examination results very creditable and the moral tone excellent'. As an old boy of the school, Lord Arundel did as old boys do, reflected on the good old days when he was a pupil. 'We', he proclaimed 'did not know what luxuries were.' They, in his day, had to get up at 6 am, go down the stone steps of St Peter's for their ablutions in a cold marble floored basement. Recent pupils, he declared, should all 'be grateful for the beautiful lavatory' which a generous management had bestowed on them. Then His Lordship proceeded to hand out the prizes 'accompanying each with a hearty handshake.' The day's events concluded with some muscular Catholicism in the form of a PT display led by Sergeant Major Philpott and, to show that the College's dramatic tradition was not forgotten, a production of *As You Like It*.

The cast of As You Like It, *performed in 1929.*

Boys' Refectory,1924.

Swimming Pool, 1924.

The Palladian Bridge and views across Bath, as seen from the steps of the Mansion.

It is thought that the advice of Capability Brown led to the construction of the Palladian Bridge in 1755. The design closely resembles bridges at Wilton and Stowe.

PHOTO BY KIND PERMISSION OF THE *BATH CHRONICLE*

The Chapel, seen from the rear. Construction began in 1844, in Roman style to harmonise with the rest of the buildings.

The new and the old can be seen together at St Mary's which accomodates boarding and day girls.

Construction of the Palladian-style Mansion began in 1737. Ralph Allen wanted not only a splendid home in which he could live in style, but he also wished to impress visitors (particularly those who might build themselves houses) with the good quality of the local stone.

St Peter's (left) was a seminary in the time of Baines, who added an extra storey in the centre, with a balustraded turret and upper lantern.

In 1834 Baines commissioned the Bath architect, H.E. Goodridge, to lay out the doubly curved stairway, before the portico, at the rear of the Mansion.

His Eminence Cardinal Cormac Murphy O'Connor STL PhL with Dr Giles Mercer KSG MA.

Ionic columns flank the front door of the Mansion.

Dr Giles Mercer and the Right Reverend Declan Lang, Bishop of Clifton, following the Headmaster's investiture with a Papal Knighthood of the Order of St Gregory. Dr Mercer is wearing his ceremonial uniform.

The Chapel, completed by 1882 to Joseph Scoles' neoclassical design, in the Roman basilican fashion of the 1840s. Fluted Corinthian pillars support a classical architrave, a frieze and a bold cornice.

Many denominations enjoy the celebration of Mass, to which all are welcome.

Off the north aisle is a series of side chapels. The Lady of the Snows is the patroness of the school.

The Kavanagh Memorial in the Chapel features a statue of St Joseph.

The Errington Corridor was built alongside the Chapel to give covered access between St Paul's and other parts of the College.

Some of the Corinthian three-quarter columns featured in the Chapel.

A statue of St Anthony of Padua is seen in a side chapel dedicated to Dr Williams.

Two of the fourteen Stations of the Cross which adorn the south wall of the Chapel.

The plasterwork in the John Wood Chapel was carefully restored following the fire of 1991.

The John Wood Chapel appears much as it would have done in the time of Allen. The wall decorations are predominantly two tiers of columns and pilasters, Corinthian above and Ionic below.

The dome above the apse of the John Wood Chapel.

The Academy Hall, seen here set out for A level examinations, contains much fine plaster-work, originally from Hunstrete House. Ornate panels depict urns, cherubs, musical instruments, flowers and garden tools among others.

One of the many fine doorways in the Mansion.

The Corinthian columns in the Entance Hall of the Mansion were added by Baines.

One of the many chandeliers. This one is in the John Wood Chapel.

The Adam-style fireplace in the Library originally came from Hunstrete House. It features the Coat of Arms of Francis Popham who owned Hunstrete.

The Bishop's Library is now used as a meeting room.

A normal school day at Prior Park.

The Swimming Pool has recently undergone major refurbishment.

PHOTO BY KIND PERMISSION OF THE *BATH CHRONICLE*

The Ball Court was restored in the 1990s. It now houses a fitness centre and is sometimes used for theatrical performances.

Prior Park as it is enjoyed today. Members of the jazz band perform on the Mansion steps and the CCF undertake a team-building exercise.

The following year the school luxuriated in the celebration of its somewhat chequered Centenary. The Archbishop of Westminster, Cardinal Bourne, presided and, for the first time, the Mansion was floodlit. Messages of congratulation were received from both the Pope and King George V. The Cardinal did in his speech what prelates tend to do and moralized: 'They could all learn a lesson from the history of Prior Park not to be discouraged by vicissitudes, nor to be cast down by any reverses.' Another guest, Dom John Chapman from Downside, graciously acknowledged the school to be 'an educational establishment of the best order'. While Alderman Jackson, the Mayor of Bath, himself not a Catholic, yet claimed that 'with the right education like that provided by the College' and with 'the exercise of that grit inherent in the British, we shall come through as a nation!' From speeches the event moved to cricket eliciting the comment of the French Catholic journal *Le Croix*, reporting on the day, that the English cannot have festival without 'une partime de cricket et la the traditionel'. Despite the Irish invasion it was all reassuringly British.

The Centenary Celebration, June 1930.

Such celebrations though worthy of note could only be the icing on the cake. What of the solid cake of school life itself? There were signs of improvement and updating of some of the buildings. Electric light was installed on the second and third floors of St Paul's while, in the early thirties, St Peter's acquired newly furbished dormitories and classrooms. St Paul's had a brand new science laboratory set up in it. In 1932 the organ in the Chapel was moved from the east end, where it had been tucked behind the high altar in the apse, to a new gallery in the west end. One of the fascinating features of this time was the school Museum which, over the years, acquired an astonishing variety of strange objects, all lovingly noted in the school magazine. Thus in 1929 the Museum receives ' an ostrich egg used in the Sudan as a water carrier, two Moorish muskets' and surely something which these days would have raised anxious eyebrows 'gelignite from HMS *Montague* wrecked off Lundy Island.' In 1930 are added 'two Jamaican machetes, seven fishing spears from the South Seas' and, revealing that there were no worries those days about a 'drug culture', 'two opium pipes'.

The washrooms in St Peter's following the installation of electric light.

St Paul's Study and Theatre in 1935.

Brother Burke.

Boys fishing on the lakes.

Ralph Allen's gift of the extensive grounds and glorious setting continued to be cared for and appreciated. In the days of financial crisis there had been a rather desperate felling of trees and selling of timber but in 1931 this began to be remedied by a burst of tree planting. The ponds in the valley became a Mecca for young anglers and in 1935 a nine-pound pike was caught along with the largest perch ever, which members of the 1st XI were able to eat for breakfast before the annual cricketing contest with Downside. In the 1930s a careful study was made of bird life in the grounds of the College. Seventy-four different species were noted, of which thirty-four were known to breed locally, including red poll, bearded tit, water rail, hooded crow and grey wagtail. The splendours of Prior Park were enough to draw 220 visiting American women graduates on an excursion in July 1932. They were said to have been 'enraptured' by it all. And they were not the only ones to come, gaze and appreciate the view. It was at this time that Queen Mary became a frequent visitor, returning time and again with other members of the royal family to share her discovery. So, although the poet Peter Levi complained of being immersed in a somewhat slanted Irish republican reading of history, the Brothers seemed to have hedged their bets and, led by Br Burke, cultivated their royal connections. The Brothers were not normally enamoured of female guests and Edith Sitwell, at this time researching her book on Bath, records that she was not allowed across the threshold of the Mansion. Clearly royal females were different.

The spiritual life of the school developed. In 1926 the great Corpus Christi procession was revived and again became quite an annual occasion for Catholics in the locality. Once a year there was a three-day Retreat for the whole College and by 1937 it was said that almost all boys were daily communicants. The solid fare of Catholic teaching and worship was embellished in ways which Bishop Baines might well have

Left: *A portrait of Queen Mary, presented to Prior Park College following one of her many visits in the 1930s.*

Below: *The royal party leaving the Mansion in 1938. Captain A Hopkins, Mayor of Bath and Rev. Br Doyle are with HM Queen Mary.*

Rev. Br Doyle, Capt A. Hopkins and HRH the Duchess of Kent during the Royal visit of 1938.

frowned at. The Apostleship of Prayer would have been acceptable but the sight of boys on the Feast of the Immaculate Conception processing carrying lilies might have caused a raised eyebrow. Yet Br Forde was insistent: ' we have not here a goody-goody set of hothouse plants, but a spirited lot that can tackle vigorously on the rugby ground, work hard in class, and yet are amenable to College discipline.' What more could a schoolmaster want? And in any case the Brothers were rather good at marking religious feasts with secular jollification. So on St Patrick's Day Mass and Benediction would be combined with cinema in the evening and on St Joseph's day with the heady delight of a whist drive. And this way of life could be said to have delivered the goods for there are some vivid little pictures of products of all this – men of quiet devoted Catholic witness. There is a senior scientist at Harwell pioneering a Mass centre there, an accountant daily at Mass in the City before going to work, the military man who, on holiday, having arrived at his hotel, had as his priority the seeking out of the nearest Catholic church – nothing fancy or spectacular here but just good solid religious practice.

School life, for the young, can seem too often to descend into grey monotony. The Brothers were alert to this, providing 'breathers', escapes from dullness. School outings were to become something of a feature of Prior Park life. In 1928 the boys set out to explore the Wye Valley. At Tintern Abbey they were greeted by rain and a guide, somewhat loftily described by one young man as 'the usual loquacious, everything off-by-heart sort of person.' The following year it was off to the seaside, to Minehead, on the feast of St Peter and St Paul, while in 1930 four large charabancs took them as far as Oxford. 'Swift as an arrow we sped on our way' but, it being a very hot day, a pause at a tea-room was as welcome as a further stop near Farringdon 'for a more delicate reason' was necessary. And when there were not outings there were organised games. If the College's cricket did not have quite the glow of the 1867–93 period, there was a great revival of rugby zealously promoted by the Irish brothers.

The School Captains, 1933. (From back left: N.P. Moynahan (Clifford), S. Hatcher-Weetman (Brownlow), H.P. Ferreira (Baines). Seated: M.F. Falkner (Captain of the School)).

Nor was it all heartiness on the sports' field. The musical tradition which Baines had established and which had been promoted by Dr Williams was to be further developed under the guidance of Norah Hodges, who was to serve Prior Park music for some forty years. An earlier music master was said to have kept half a cricket bat up a chimney with which to chastise any young musician who played a false note but Norah Hodges's gentler ways seem to have been as effective. There she is in 1927 lecturing on 'The Orchestra' with musical illustrations on the latest 'HMV gramophone lent by Messrs Milsom of Bath.' Neither was drama forgotten despite the fact that an actor, Mr Macready, visiting the College with his wife to lecture on the Theatre, gave the dire warning 'Never take to the stage as a profession!' But by this time Seymour Hicks who, as we have already seen, was converted to the profession by Prior Park, was providing counter-evidence. By the twenties he was an established actor on both stage and screen. And there were other old boys who followed him in this career, notably Patrick Kirwan and Horace Vachell, and the College itself was poised to enjoy a new flourishing of the drama. But now of course there were new experiences to be had. A growing interest in the 'wireless' is reported and in response the establishment of Prior Park Radio Society. Then as Seymour Hick's career suggests, there was the birth and

Horace Annesley Vachell.

Sir Seymour Hicks.

First XV 1928

Back: *F.J. Lauder, T. O'C. Sinnott, J.M. Ossorio, M.C. Curtis, R.J. Oates, G.M. White, D.W. Dixie.* Middle: *J.B. O'Donovan, A.A. More O'Ferrall, J.J. Baldwin (Capt), W.W. Oates (Vice Capt), J.A. Daly, G.A. Kelly.* Seated: *T.D. England, B.F. England.*

Prior Park XI 1928

J.P. Sutton, R.J. Oates, R.D. Sullivan, J.B. O'Donovan, D.W. Dixie, T.P. Ralls, W.G. Devanney, W.W. Oates (Vice Capt), J.J. Baldwin (Capt), W.P. Ryan, G.A. Kelly, T.D. England, B.F. England.

rise of the cinema and from 1928 the boys were to enjoy two hours film entertainment each week. At first the films were silent so the showing of 'The Battle of the Falkland Islands' was accompanied by Gillet and Seal on the piano, and 'Fleet meets Fleet' with appropriate music 'rendered by Miss N. Hodges LRAM.'

The Brothers seem to have seen it as part of their vocation to teach raw youths some of the finer points of social life. Kevin Tyndall, writing on the Thirties at Prior Park, recalls sessions on Saturday mornings at which 'Manners and Etiquette' were taught by Br Burke. The injunction that 'a gentleman opens the door for his lady to enter before him into their dwelling, but precedes her when they are leaving' was explained by the need to guard the lady from villains as she enters and going out before her by the need 'to ensure that it is safe for her to follow'. As these lessons were drawn from a textbook of the nineteenth century, it is not surprising that the instruction that gentlemen accompanying a lady in the street should 'always walk on the outside' is explained by the necessity of shielding 'the lady's long dress from being splashed by horses' hooves.' It is also not surprising that, even in 1938, all this was received with some bemused hilarity.

Rev. Br W.D. Forde, the Mayor of Bath, the Bishop of Clifton, the Rt Hon. J.A. Lyons, Premier of Australia, Rev. Br E.B. Doyle, the Mayoress of Bath, Dame Enid Lyons and Miss Sheila Lyons, pictured outside the Mansion.

Life at Prior Park was certainly not all work, or even all prayer; a diverse sporting and cultural life was developing. Schools tend to become isolated little islands which breed an over-solemnity with the trivial round, so news of former pupils in different walks of life can throw open a few windows and set all this in a wider context. There are stories of old Canon Hazeland at the age of eighty-four, still coming to take the waters in Bath, plodding up the hill to the College and back in order to save money. News came of the death of Professor Samuel George Shattock after a long and distinguished career in morbid anatomy. Three American pupils, Miguel, Luis, and Jose Ossorio had gone on from Prior Park to Harvard. Anthony Thompson wrote enthusiastically in the school magazine of the importance of a more scientifically educated farming profession and C.S. Williams was becoming an equally ardent evangelist for Engineering while Frank Walsh, the neurologist, was appointed editor of the journal *Brain*. Prior Park continued to realise the

Guests at Speech Day, 1931 were: Seated: *Lord Arundel of Wardour, Rt Rev. Mgr Provost Lee VG, Rev. Br W.D. Forde, President, Rt Rev. Abbot White CRL.* Standing: *Mr Austin King KSG, Mr J.J. Bridge HMI, Very Rev. Canon Sugden.*

The FIRST XV 1934

Standing: *D.M. Fleming, W.P. Foster, G.E. Leigh, L.B. O'Reilly, J.W. Marmion, F.H. Fox, J.H. O'Neill, J.H. Sloan.* Sitting: *F.M. Falkner, S.P. Clements (Vice Capt), J.D. Williams (Capt), J.L. Pardoe, I.A. Lee.* In front: *A.G. de Freitas, M.F. Knight.*

aims of its founder by producing a steady flow of candidates for the priesthood. In 1934 it had seminarians at the English College in Rome, St Sulpice in Paris, Valladolid in Spain and back home at Ushaw in Co Durham and Oscott in Birmingham, together with candidates for priesthood in both the Dominican and Franciscan orders. In 1933 there is reported the death of Captain C.H. Cardovo who had been a pupil from 1887-93. Wounded in the First World War he had tried to settle in Devon but in search of the sun ended up at St Cyr-sur-Loire where as 'a musician of note' and 'of a very social disposition', he was able to display his gifts which were said to be' of the drawing room and of the club rather then of the sports field.' It takes all sorts to make a truly Catholic college.

A photograph taken outside the Old Pavilion, at an Old Boys v the School cricket match.

While the windows of school life opened up into the activities of its former pupils so too they continued to open into the life of the Diocese of Clifton. Although no longer a diocesan college, friendly relations with the local church still mattered so, when an old friend Mgr William Lee became the Bishop of Clifton, Prior Park rejoiced. It was sad that some wounds of the past were re-opened with the publication of Br Roche's great history of the College. The heavyweight Downside historian Cuthbert Butler thundered that Roche had whitewashed Bishop Baines 'at the cost of blackwashing others.' 'History is history', he wrote in the *Downside Review* 'and facts are facts, and the idealization of Bishop Baines's personality cannot be effected without reacting disadvantageously on the memory of other good men.' The *Times Literary Supplement* was gentler on the author but rather more disparaging on the reputation of the College declaring that 'every church has its educational skeletons, and the Roman Catholic Church in England has had Prior Park, which converts used to hear discussed with bated breath and muffled curses.' However, whatever raw nerves Br Roche's book had touched, enough harmony was restored for the College to join happily with other Catholics on 19 May 1935 to celebrate the canonization of the martyrs John Fisher and Thomas More.

A Press Officer at a Prior Park sports day in the 1930s.

But there pressed upon the College's life not only the downs and ups of ecclesiastical life, but also those of a nation moving through the greyness of the post-war economic depression with its high unemployment. At Speech Day in 1933 there were references to 'these difficult times' and in 1934 it was openly acknowledged that 'the economic difficulties of the present time' had led to some pupils having to withdraw from the College. It was recognised that bursaries were really needed to provide for such times of economic embarrassment. A peep of this darker social scene was given to pupils as they could see a squad of the unemployed clearing the ground in the valley around the Palladian Bridge. There was a public darkening of a different nature as the College joined with the nation in 1936 to mourn the death of King George V. The school magazine for July of that year looks forward with confidence to the reign of his successor Edward VIII – 'the grief occasioned by his passing has been somewhat assuaged by the knowledge that his son and successor King Edward VIII ascends to the throne in the affection of his subjects. The immense popularity he has won as Prince of Wales and the ability and tact he has shown in various diplomatic and other missions presage a very successful reign for our new king.' In view of this confidence proving rather swiftly to be misplaced, it is perhaps understandable that the school magazine passes over the events of the abdication in silence and only rejoins the narrative with the College enjoying a day off in 1937 to celebrate the Coronation of Edward's brother as King George VI.

With the leaders of the Empire and Commonwealth gathering for this Coronation there came Prime Minister Lyons from Australia. Br Burke, always with an eye for the great and good, made sure that this Catholic leader, whose twelve children had been educated by the Christian Brothers, should pay a visit to Prior Park. So it was arranged that he and his wife should be the guests of honour at Prize Day and they clearly both went down well with the College. The boys were charmed by Lady Lyons while the Brothers were well content with the fulsome tribute which the Prime Minister paid to their Congregation for its great work in the development of secondary education in Australia.

Going home.

Cricket team, 1929
Back row: *W.R. Canning (scorer), L.C. Ossorio, G.A. Kelly, M.C. Curtis, J.M. Ossorio, J. Sutton (umpire).* Middle: *D.W. Dixie, J.A. Daly, W.W. Oates (captain), R.J. Oates, J.B. O'Donovan.* Front: *T.D. England (Vice Captain), B.F. England.*

PRIOR PARK UNDER FIRE

For those with eyes to see the shadows of war in Europe were again gathering. Although Prior Park had not, as a school community, lived through the 1914-18 War, its old boys certainly had, so, along with all other schools, it carried its scars in the shape of those memorial tablets which spoke louder than words of that appalling loss of young life. Armistice Day 11 November was every year a poignant occasion solemnly observed. Even those who had escaped with their lives by no means escaped unscathed. Many were damaged physically or mentally. Sir Denzil Cope was said to have had 'his nerves shattered by all the scenes of suffering he saw.' His experiences gave him 'an intense feeling for the suffering of humanity' which he would gather and offer up in his daily attendance at Mass. The shrinking of the survivors of that war from the very thought of another one cannot be underestimated. An uncle of the writer had been a Navigator with the Flying Corps, was shot down and endured the privations of a prisoner of war. His nerves were also shattered and, unable to face the prospect of another war, took his own life. As the shadow became clearer and ever more unavoidable, there was an edge to the College's 11 November commemoration, as it gathered for the silence and the recitation of the psalm De Profundis.

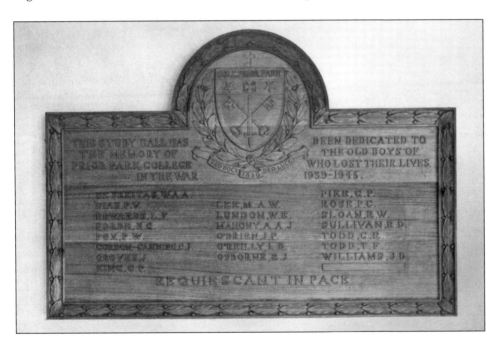

The memorial to those who died in the Second World War which is in the Chapel at Prior Park.

But how aware was the little world of Prior Park of this threat? How were young Catholics viewing the rise of Mussolini in Italy, of Hitler in Germany and what did they make of Franco's overthrow of the democratically elected government of Spain? Stephen Weetman, then a seminarian at the English College in Rome, wrote: 'Fascism, amongst the many good things it achieved, caused the Church once more to be respected.' This was, of course, after Mussolini had exchanged his early virulent anti-ecclesiastical views for the practical wisdom of seeking a

The College in the early days of the war.

more peaceable accommodation with the Vatican. This was achieved by the Lateran Treaty of 11 February 1929. *L'Osservatore Romano* declared that through this Treaty 'Italy has been given back to God and God to Italy.' Certainly the relationship established by it seemed to be of advantage to both parties. It is hardly surprising that a seminarian, who later became a much respected and loved lay teacher at the College, should, at this time, be flirting with Fascism. After all many others were doing the same and there was the respected Catholic weekly *The Tablet* declaring 'the great hearted' Mussolini to have 'shown himself an intellectual giant' and Pope Pius XI calling the dictator 'the man whom Providence has sent.' When the highly successful black athlete Jessie Owens was booed by the Nazi racist crowd at the Berlin Olympics in 1936, which was thought to have been 'the most unpleasant crowd before which athletes have had to compete', Prior

Speech Day prizewinners from 1937.

Park magazine provided an apologist. These complaints, wrote one old boy, were a great exaggeration 'admittedly the succession of Negro victories must have been galling to a German crowd, but if Jesse Owens and others did not get a welcoming roar, they were certainly greeted with polite if perfunctory clapping'! Another old boy, M.T. Coyne travelling in the Rhineland as late as 1938, claimed that the German people were not interested in politics and commended 'the delightful cleanliness of Germany' which compared favourably with what he called 'the squalor' of Belgium. In 1939 there came the sad report that two old boys, Jose Frois and Felipe Berge, had been killed in action fighting under Franco in the Spanish Civil War.

All this reflects the rather uncritical Catholic dalliance with right-wing extremism of that period. This clearly sprang from the perception that the real threat was the Red menace of the Soviet Union. All enemies of the USSR, it seemed, must be friends of the Church. Moreover were not these dictators providing just what an authoritarian church insisted that people needed – order and firm discipline? Had not Pius XI favoured what he called 'Catholic totalitarianism' and were not 'family values' safer under Mussolini than any government of the left? Catholics bred for heel-clicking obedience to absolute church authority failed to detect some of the maggots in these apples, for instance that Mussolini, while discovering the uses of being a Catholic, saw none in being a Christian. The startling distinction in his mind is instructive. Christianity, he rightly perceived, inescapably had its roots in Judaism and that he could not be having. Hitler, with his naked neo-paganism, was always more difficult for Catholics to take, while Franco, like Mussolini, was easier. Faced with the appalling slaughter of priests and nuns by the left in Spain, it was at least tempting to turn a blind eye to Franco's ruthless use of torture and executions and throw in one's lot with this version of 'Catholic totalitarianism'. As we have heard in our own time, cannot a few human rights be traded in for the sake of security and national unity? So when the College debated the motion 'Dictatorship is superior to Democracy' it was not surprising that the latter won by only the narrowest of margins.

But not even the clouds of euphoria emanating from the Lateran Pact could altogether dispel those of war. The school magazine carried an article on how to lay sea mines and gave news of Dennis Branigan engaged in building destroyers at Cowes. Although Seymour Hicks played the 'cheerful chappie' seeing it to be a 'duty to be merry' and exhorting his contemporaries to 'join the laughing optimists', in September 1938 the College had to come down to earth and face the serious business of fitting gas masks. But then in a trice these could be laid aside for had not Prime Minister Neville Chamberlain come back from Munich waving his piece of paper and assuring all that there would be 'peace in our time'? Prior Park, along with most of the nation, was eager to believe the good news. On 19 October the College Debating Society added its endorsement of the policy of

The Brownlow House team with the Inter House Debating Trophy 1938.

PRIOR PARK COLLEGE

PRESENTS

JOURNEY'S END

by

R. C. SHERRIFF

November 25th – 28th, 1953

Programme 6d.

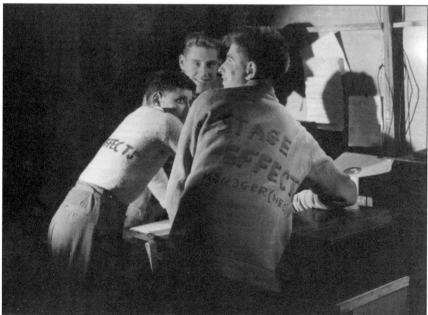

CAST
(in order of appearance)

Captain Hardy	...	PAUL DOYLE
Lieutenant Osborne	...	PETER SCOTT
Private Mason	...	BRENDON O'DRISCOLL
Lance Corporal Broughton	...	DERMOT MURRAY
2nd Lieutenant Raleigh	...	PETER HUTCHINGS
Captain Stanhope	...	NICHOLAS TRANTER
2nd Lieutenant Trotter	...	JAMES PEDEN
A Runner	...	JOHN HAMMOND
2nd Lieutenant Hibbert	...	MALCOLM DRURY
The Company Sergeant Major	...	MICHAEL MULCAHY
The Colonel	...	JAMES NORRIS
A German Soldier	...	MICHAEL HELY

Journey's End, performed in 1953.

appeasement by overwhelmingly passing the motion 'Mr Chamberlain deserves well of his country'. So it was back to life as usual. A Philatelic Society was founded and the school museum acquired a lump of lava from Vesuvius, some mosquitoes (dead) from Shanghai and silkworm cocoons from Milan. As if to crown this mood of reassurance old Queen Mary visited the College again, this time accompanied by the Duchess of Kent to whom the seven-year-old Peter Levi presented a bouquet of flowers said to be 'nearly as large as himself.' All things must be well.

Some of the old boys though were waking up to reality. A group came to the College to debate with the young on the issue of compulsory National Service in the armed forces. The pupils seemed altogether more complacent than their elders whom they judged to be 'suffering from nerves' and whom they rebuked for seeming 'to think war inevitable.' With a Government 'alert and mentally fit' the younger generation saw no need of National Service – 'the voluntary scheme' they loftily declared 'was sufficient'. It took an old boy at the Prior Park Association dinner to declare: 'Today we are living in the age of Hitler and things are by no means as safe as houses.'

All of which, of course, was to prove to be the case in the following year. 1939 began with heavy snow, the delight of every schoolboy, so there was the excitement of snow balling and tobogganing in the valley. On 10 February Pope Pius XI died and the school gathered around the wireless to listen to his Funeral and again, after the election of his successor Pacelli as Pius XII, to the papal Coronation Mass. But during the school summer holidays the nation went to war and the College came back for the autumn term praying 'for victory of right over wrong.' This year there was to be no Guy Fawkes party on 5 November and the Armistice Day celebrations a few days later seemed 'particularly depressing' as they gathered 'to remember those who gave their lives in the war to end war.'

This was the period of the so-called 'phoney war' when nothing much seemed to happen. 'War', the school magazine rather jauntily proclaimed, 'does not seem to press heavily on the nerves but provides many topics of conversation.' Yet the authorities had to admit that the time had come to 'tackle the blackout business seriously' and the first trial air raid assembly was held. The war was also to impinge on the end of term arrangements. Boys travelling by train were confronted by an 'emergency' rail timetable so had to rise to catch what was available at what they described with distaste as 'an unearthly hour'. But still, before the term ended, spirits were raised by a concert organised by the indefatigable Norah Hodges and the newly-acquired elocution master Hedley Goodall. It starred Peter Levi as Snow White.

During 1940 the reality of war was inescapable. Out in Buenos Aires Dr Michael Petty found himself having to tend the wounded of HMS *Exeter* and HMS *Ajax* after their clash with the *Graf Spee*. Michael Rea, a seminarian at St Sulpice in Paris, was hurriedly evacuated to Bordeaux, while the ebullient Seymour Hicks was appointed controller of ENSA, the body devoted to bringing entertainment and good cheer to British troops throughout the world. The New Year began with bitter cold. On 21 January 20 degrees of frost were recorded and by the 29th trees were splitting with frost and the telegraph wires were down. Without the telephone and shivering in the cold, the College felt like the nation, bleak and isolated. There was even the admission that 'vitality had been brought to a low pitch'. Br Doyle's sepulchral words captured the mood – 'darkness has descended on

Europe. The old world is in an appalling condition. Treachery and injustice, death and destruction are abroad.' Yet staff and pupils braced themselves and embarked upon an activity which was to become central to school life during the war, the collecting and chopping of firewood.

At this time of national crisis a typical school worry arose – with the nation 'engaged in a life and death struggle' was it really appropriate to hold a Speech Day? In the end it was decided that the path of duty decreed that the event should go ahead precisely to defy any 'mood of defeatism' and to show publicly that Prior Park at least would not let 'the war get us down.' So the presiding Bishop Lee was able confidently to announce that 'God would give us victory in the war because what were we fighting for but the recognition of him and his Kingdom?' And then to show that the College itself was 'doing its bit' for the war effort, he announced that the new teaching block had been handed over for the duration of the war 'to the Civil Service to help them continue the great work they are doing for us and for our world.' Behind all of which lies a story, told by the late Mgr Jim Kelly with some gusto, which speaks volumes about the character of Bishop Lee.

Brothers Forde and Doyle in conspiratorial mood.

Way back in 1939 the warning had been given that Prior Park might have to be requisitioned or made to share its site with a Catholic girls' secondary school. The Bishop and the Brothers united to object to both proposals. Indeed, if anything the prospect of the dilution of this all-male world seemed more dreadful than that of requisitioning. For a while both fates were avoided. But in February 1940 Sir Patrick Duff of the Office of Works wrote of the Admiralty's great need for further accommodation in Bath where it was now based. The threat was no longer a distant one. Seeing this Bishop Lee promptly moved into action. Sweeping up Br Doyle, and armed with a cunning plan in his head and a bottle of whisky in his bag, the Bishop and the Brother embarked upon the train to London, there to confront the Minister in his lair. Battling his way firmly through secretaries to the august presence, the Bishop presented his case. Was not the nation, he argued, eager for the United States to come to the Allies' aid at this time? But, as the Minister well knew, there were many Roman Catholics in that country and it would not play well with them if it were known that the British Government had closed down a leading Catholic school. Of course the College was more than eager to do anything in its power to assist the war effort and, as it happened, there was a brand new teaching block in the process of being built but this process had ground to a standstill because of wartime building restrictions. Were the Minister able to lift these restrictions then, of course, the Admiralty would have for its use a brand new building. What could be better? The Minister saw the wisdom of the Bishop's plan and agreed to a solution which provided government with what it needed, saved the College from being requisitioned and ensured the completion of the new teaching block – all of course in the national interest. So the Bishop was able to produce from his bag that bottle of whisky to celebrate with the Minister such a happy arrangement!

The pace of war increased during 1940. On 26 May there was a much needed national Day of Prayer for the British Expeditionary Force in Flanders. On 10 June Italy joined Germany in the war against the Allies and on 25 June at 12.30 am Prior Park experienced its first air raid warning. As the threat became real, beds were moved in St Paul's to the ground floor. The imposition of Double Summer Time, as a means of what they called 'daylight saving', meant even darker winter mornings. This in turn, for an institution with such large buildings, presented difficult 'black-out' problems. How was the school to satisfy sharp-eyed ARP wardens and

The Corpus Christi celebrations of 1941.

prevent its conspicuously sited buildings from becoming a beacon for incoming enemy bombers? The problem was solved by a simple adjustment to the school's day, which was now to start an hour later.

Against this gloomy background, the Debating Society had a re-run of its 1938 debate on Chamberlain's policy of appeasement. Suffice it to say that the school's earlier favourable judgement was decisively reversed and nobody seemed to have a good word to say for the unfortunate Neville Chamberlain. Despite Bishop Lee's careful playing of the American card in his encounter with Sir Patrick Duff, the same Debating Society concluded that 'it was not advantageous to England for the USA to enter war on our side.' The very thought of England being in need of outside help seemed to be distinctly unpatriotic. A further curious debate was held at this time on the motion that 'up to now the war has brought more good than evil to the country'. Those who held this bracing view pointed out that the war had at least solved the unemployment problem, brought national unity, 'ensured thrift, a balanced diet, sound living and high thinking' – above all it had 'raised interest in religion'. However, those who took the contrary view bemoaned the damage being done to the fabric of society. Social barriers were being swept away, there was an increased 'tendency to socialism' and heavy burdens of taxation had been laid upon the people.

News of old boys became increasingly news of their lives and deaths. Early in the war the DFC was awarded to Flt Lt Billy Drake. He was to prove one of those rare pilot war heroes, ever more decorated for his gallantry, who lived to survive the hostilities. John Banwell, an ambulance driver, had a close escape at Dunkirk. But not so lucky were Pilot Officer Ralph Osborne, Maurice Lee and Bob Sloane. The latter died just ten days after his twenty-first birthday and a week after his wedding. Brian Smith who was a pupil at that time recalls Br Hayes having to make frequent formal announcements of the deaths of former pupils, to which would always be added a prayer for the repose of their souls. On the home front the war drew nearer. In January 1941, planes returning from one of those many Bristol raids off-loaded incendiary bombs which fell close to the Palladian Bridge. That was followed in May by a high-explosive bomb, which never went off but left a large crater a few yards from the same bridge. But there were consolations both of a secular and spiritual nature. Queen Mary, by now evacuated to Badminton, paid her fourth visit to the College, this time accompanied by the Princess Royal and Viscount Lascelles. The Corpus Christi celebrations of 1941 were actually bigger and better than ever. This was mainly due to the presence of ever-larger numbers of Convent girls flooding in from schools which had been evacuated to the Bath area. Whatever the Brothers may have feared from the propinquity of the feminine, the boys seem to have appreciated it.

Before dispersing for the Easter holidays in 1942, the College celebrated Palm Sunday as a day of Prayer for Peace. So it was mercifully, while the boys were on holiday, that there came the great Bath raids over the weekend of April 25 and 26. Br Doyle describes how on the Saturday evening the sirens sounded at 11.20pm. Nobody thought much about it for by now this had become a fairly usual occurrence with German bombers passing constantly on their way to Bristol. But with the ever-present possibility of stray bombs falling as they had done in the recent past, Brothers Doyle, Roche and Ryan were dispatched to their usual posts on the Portico to keep an eye on things. Gunfire was to be heard over the eastern approaches to the city and within three minutes something ominously unusual happened – flares began to descend over Bath. That was the moment when the fire-watchers realised that they were in for more than a few stray bombs for the flares showed that Bath itself was being targeted. Alarm bells were set ringing throughout the College and Br O'Connell was dispatched to the lodge to warn Mr Gregory, the caretaker, and his family. Just as the Brother was returning, a bomb exploded on the grass bank outside St Paul's. Meanwhile Br Burke, never a man to be unduly disturbed by air raid warnings, was sitting in his room in St Paul's. He had ignored the ringing bells and was quietly absorbed in his correspondence. Within a trice he found the ceilings descending on him, the door blown across the room and the windows blown out. The Brother emerged unscathed. Ten minutes later another cluster of bombs fell, one a hundred yards below St Peter's and two in the big lake. This first Bath raid continued until 5.15 the following morning.

Bomb damage to St Paul's.

Br Doyle writes of the aftermath: 'At dawn there was an opportunity of seeing something of the damage. It was found that every window in St Paul's, in the College Chapel and in the Errington Corridor was blown into tiny pieces. The eastern half of the steps outside St Paul's was blown up and the balustrading about these steps had totally disintegrated.' The balcony over the entrance to St Paul's was destroyed. Inside, the ceilings were down in the Errington Corridor leading to St Paul's and in what were then called the 'Arcades', the area which has now been converted into the Roche Housemaster's flat. The ceiling of the south aisle of the Chapel was down as was most of its roof. In St Paul's itself there was damage to the roof and to the dormitories – 'ceilings were down, the walls cracked and the doors wrenched from their jambs'. Across the way the brand new teaching block suffered similar blast damage.

The following night there were further raids on Bath. The Brothers watched from the portico 'hundreds of incendiary bombs bursting into flame on the North Western side of the City.' The raid this time lasted just over an hour and the College escaped further damage. But down in Bath there was devastation. It is estimated that some 275 tonnes of bombs were dropped on the Bath area during these two nights, 2495 buildings were destroyed or seriously damaged, 400 people were killed and 357 badly injured. Out at the Haycombe Cemetery a sombre line of headstones can be seen marking where 207 of the victims were buried. Four churches were completely destroyed and, included among the further seven badly damaged, was St John's Catholic Church which had received a direct hit on the presbytery. Two curates stood together that night, Fr Sheridan and Fr Jim Kelly. As they saw the mayhem closing in these two priests gave each other conditional absolution. When the bomb dropped Fr Sheridan was killed along with the housekeeper and her family. Fr Kelly used to tell the tale of how he was at once dispatched by his Parish Priest to the Police Station, then in Orange Grove where Brown's restaurant now is, to inform the authorities of the situation at St John's. Through fire and falling masonry Fr Kelly advanced to the station desk with his news. Not to be ruffled or hustled the Sergeant simply replied: 'Well Sir, we shall want that in writing!'

Back up at Prior Park the Brothers gave thanks that the boys had been away on holiday and then set to work to restore some order to the chaos. It meant 'covering up what was left of the window frames with cloth and making and hanging temporary doors.' These were the days when teachers were expected to be able to turn their hands to almost any task. By the end of two weeks they were able to inform parents that the College would be able to re-open on 15 May. All pupils duly reported back on that day. Naturally it was not a very easy term. Washing arrangements were complicated and classrooms draughty. But it was mercifully the summer term and the weather was good. Moreover schoolboys actually enjoy some disruption of the deadly order of school routine. The Mayor of Bath made a point of visiting the College to congratulate it on 'playing their part in the war effort' with such 'grit and determination.' But not surprisingly the Corpus Christi celebrations in June had to be somewhat cut down.

As the school magazine put it, the war continued 'to inflict itself on us at every hand's turn. Not a day passes that its horrors, its griefs, its inconveniencies do not loom large.' Pupils from this era speak with feeling of the cold and hunger they suffered. Rationing was severe and school food austere. Approach to the Refectory was heralded, a contemporary writes, 'with the odours of boiled cabbage, culinary garbage and domestic smells'. At breakfast there was porridge, which had 'the

Sodality of Mary Immaculate.
Back row: P.R. Lechy, A. Cotter,
S.P. Clements, J.L. Pardoe,
P.M. McKeigue, A. De Feitas.
Seated: T.J. Hughes, S. Hatcher-
Weetman, N.P. Moynahan, H.P.
Ferreira.

consistency of rubber' which was followed by something cooked, a sausage maybe or a rasher of bacon or a few slices of polony from the famed Bath pork butchers Spears. The breakfast highlight of the week was the Sunday hot pork pie from that same shop. At midday there was the main meal of such delights as corned beef fritters or fish pie made from herrings in tomato sauce. All was accompanied by lashings of overcooked vegetables. Some judged that it was the cooking which actually made the food so unappetising. For tea there was bread and a pat of margarine with the same for supper but with a glass of milk instead of tea. The writer remembers at this time eating such a school supper, though with hot cocoa rather than milk, while doing his prep. Drops of melted margarine had to be kept from sullying the Latin prose. Such a diet was supplemented by 'tuck' brought from or sent by post from home. These were typically things like pickles, golden syrup, baked beans and cake.

It was of this period in the College's life that the poet Peter Levi wrote in his auto-biographical fragment *The Flutes of Autumn*. This was the time when he and his contemporaries met and chatted with the parachutists camped on the cricket field just before Arnhem. With his brother Anthony, Peter Levi had been sent to Prior Park before the war. He was then aged six! Their father took them on a tour of Catholic schools. Stonyhurst, he thought, looked like a prison while it was rumoured that at Beaumont the young took to drink. In the end it had to be Prior Park, which won purely in virtue of its magically wonderful setting. It was from this that the future poet reckoned that he had received his most important education in landscape, architecture and wild flowers. Here was 'an artificial paradise running gently to seed'.

But he found nothing gentle in the rest of his schooling. 'The landscape I loved with a passion' but the Brothers he came to hate. 'What did I hate about the Brothers so much?' he asks and replies that it was 'the scrubbed, healthy, uncomprehending faces of the younger ones, the touches of Catholic anti-Semitism, their fanatical hatred of female sexuality, their physical intolerance. They differed from the school bullies in a school where bullying was as organized as mealtimes, only in age and authority.' The history and the politics, which the Brothers taught, Levi judged to be 'wickedly prejudiced and crazy.' Brian Smith, a contemporary, also found the teaching left much to be desired. 'Learning' he writes 'was very much by rote and one was made to learn by the threat of a whack on your hand if you didn't. We were not given the opportunity to think or reason for ourselves and I left school with virtually no knowledge of music, the arts, economics or politics.' It was not until after the war in 1947 when Sidney Ash joined as a lay member of staff, that he says that he encountered 'the first teacher that I ever remembered who treated me as an intelligent person in my own right.' And Smith echoes Levi's judgement on the Brothers fear of sexuality. 'There was no sex education at that time' he writes and adds that they were 'constantly told that perfection in life was to become a celibate priest.'

The young Levi was bullied and bored. And that is what drove him to escape 'into the woods, to hide and to read and read' or 'run away to Bath to the junk shops and tea shops, the Dickensian back streets and the architecture.' The charge of 'brutality and boredom' will ring bells with many of those who had to live through public school education at this time. In truth the war and post-war period were times of cold, hunger, inadequate teaching, and unbelievable dreariness. With most young and able men away in the services, tired and sometimes rather deranged old men manned the teaching barricades and proved only too willing to delegate responsibility for discipline and order to mindless thugs who were turned into prefects. Life tended to be nasty, brutish and alas not short. Once the younger men emerged from the war and were fed into the system, for most schools there was a dramatic change for the better. The trouble is that such excuses cannot be really made in the case of Prior Park. The younger Brothers were sturdily Irish and therefore safe from recruitment to the British forces.

Brian Smith's judgement of the Brothers is somewhat more genial than is Levi's. Even Br Dunne who dispatched class miscreants into the stationery cupboard with the cry 'Into the Press!' seems to have been redeemed by his passion for cards which made him turn the Saturday morning RI lesson into an opportunity to introduce the boys to contract bridge. Br Hayes, known to the boys as Daisy, was a fierce censor of magazines being especially careful to cut out the daily Jane strip in the *Mirror* and even advertisements for ladies' underwear, but Brian Smith found him a kind man, who of an evening would sit with them before a blazing fire to talk to them over their hot Oxo. Although he had a sharp and fierce eye for any bullying, other juvenile misbehaviour would as likely have him rubbing his forehead in despair, crying 'Boys, boys, boys!' Certainly there were those touches of staff eccentricity which often make school life tolerable for the young. There was the lay teacher, the bald-headed, shortsighted Mr Kenny who owned a budgerigar which accompanied him in a cage to meals and to classes. The fact that he and Br Hayes had a long-standing feud only added a touch of spice to it all. Mr Miller, the industrial chemist, who, because none of the Brothers was able to teach the subject, came to the school two evenings a week to teach Chemistry to a select few, was fondly remembered for his 'fund of dirty jokes' which accompanied a brew up of Heinz tomato soup over a Bunsen burner. Brian Smith recalls that the soup acquired a slight flavouring of hydrochloric acid.

But the casual brutality and generally uncivilized nature of the school, which Peter Levi found, was certainly not unique to the world of the Christian Brothers. However, many for whom these days bring painful memories were grateful to

W.G. de Freitas seen outside St Paul's before the war.

find a safety valve, for in a society in which while clear dangers came from outside, life within was quite secure for the young. This meant that they did not have to be for ever watched and controlled with anxious care so that there were opportunities to escape from the restrictions and the hardships, to explore whether the countryside or the fascinations of town and city.

The war continued to take a more terrible toll on former members of the College. Wing Commander Wilfred de Freitas was killed in the Libyan campaign and William Edward Lundan flying his Hurricane crashed to his death. Late in the war in the Far East, Bernard Ward was to die in the storming of Mandalay, while Major James D. Williams was killed in Burma. Of course there were those who escaped unscathed and increasingly be-medalled. Billy Drake earned a bar to his DFC, while Major John Burnett won both the DSC and MC for his intelligence work in Burma. Another upon whom fortune smiled was Lt Denis Gilmer who, having, as one of the Desert Rats battled in tanks in North Africa, then had to fight

Denis Gilmer, who was later to become a Desert Rat, photographed outside the Old Pavilion.

Lt Col Walter Raleigh Chichester OBE JP.

The first post-war dinner of the Prior Park Association.

up through Italy. As time went by things distinctly improved for him. The school magazine was able to report that he 'has changed residence from sleeping in tanks, tents and less commodious abodes in the African desert for a fine billet' and finally, when the war ended, it finds him living it up in some well-deserved luxury near Lake Como.

Back at the College there was still time to debate the value of the 'old school tie'. Supporters of the said tie were clear that class distinctions should be carefully preserved for, they argued, 'authority comes naturally to the sons of the well-to-do' and were not all good 'Empire builders, old school tie men?' It is re-assuring that there were those who could see through this comfortable belief and challenge a tradition 'fostered by the rich to fool the masses'. 'Intelligence and merit' it was argued 'should be the key to advancement, not money and social position.' Was it a straw in the wind, a sign of changing attitudes that it was these critics of the 'old school tie' who won the debate? For, of course, the war came to an end to signal something of a social revolution. The hero Winston Churchill was swept from office in the 1945 General Election and Clement Attlee led a reforming Labour Government. What would the future now be for those 'old school tie' assumptions and for places like Prior Park which nurtured them?

But now for the moment time was made to celebrate the nation's victory in Europe in May 1945. Those celebrations tended to be limited by the austerities of the day. The author's prep school managed to lay on batter puddings and golden syrup for breakfast and an extra opportunity to bathe in the afternoon. Prior Park ran to a Missa Cantata in thanksgiving for victory and a chanted Te Deum on the Sunday after VE Day. Brian Smith writes: 'we had a day off school and we descended on Bath in the morning, not that there was much to do as it was a general holiday and the shops were shut'. In the evening there was a bonfire and the setting off of some fireworks. Billy Drake DFC with bar, DSO, DFM with eleven other pilots led the vanguard of 300 aircraft in the flight over London to commemorate the Battle of Britain. An emaciated Leslie Budding emerging from a Japanese POW camp was a visible reminder of the cost of it all.

THE POST WAR RECOVERY

T he post-war period proved to be a time of continuing hardship. It is often forgotten that food rationing was even tighter after the war, involving the introduction of bread rationing for the first time. As the demands of a reviving industry grew and with service in the armed forces continuing to create a shortage of coal miners, this was also a time of grave fuel shortages. And that mattered because the winters of the late forties were bitterly cold. 1947 saw scenes of arctic weather. The River Avon froze over at the Cleveland Bridge. Memories of all who were at school in those days are dominated by hunger and cold. Prior Park's misery was intensified that year by the tragic death of a thirteen-year-old pupil William Morris from meningitis.

Members of St Paul's, 1946.

Along with all these discomforts there was the ongoing problem of the bomb damage to St Paul's. Patching up was the best that could be done as rebuilding priority in Bath had rightly to be given to those who had lost their homes during the blitz. Officialdom was parsimonious in handing out building permits and few came the College's way. Speech Day accounts of College life are full of lamentations about the difficulty of satisfying a growing demand for places in the school with so much of the St Paul's building out of action. Every now and again hopes are raised that 'by next year' the work will be completed only to find those hopes dashed. It was all very frustrating.

Yet life went on, driven by the gritty determined quality of the Christian Brothers and this life was not entirely grey – there were modest entertainments – a whist drive on St Patrick's Day and, on the Feast of SS Peter and Paul, 'an instructional film on the manufacture of high grade steel.' There was even a revival of the annual school outing although, with petrol rationing still tight, it was only possible to take the boys as far as Cheddar and Wells. Perhaps one sees creeping in a

Peter Packwood tries out a home-made sledge on the bank in front of St Paul's in the winter of 1947.

St Paul's following restoration.

An outing to Stonehenge.

touch of modernity in that members of the 6th Form were allowed to share with the girls' school in Oldfield Park a film on tennis. As far as one can see, this, with the exception of tantalising glimpses at the Corpus Christi procession, is the first recorded introduction of the boys to a female world.

As the Labour Government forged ahead with its radical programme for the Welfare State and the nationalization of the railways and the coal mining industry, Br Roche shook his head. In 1949 he criticised the extravagance of the 'modern welfare state' – it all meant 'everything for nothing' he lamented. The proceedings of the Debating Society reveal that the College generally was not a hotbed of left-wing subversion. Even after a war against the dictators, democracy was judged not to be 'the best form of government' and the restraining power of the House of Lords was strongly supported. The dropping of the atomic bombs on Japan caused no stirrings of Catholic conscience. This carnage seemed amply justified. And, as for proposals to abolish the death penalty or to build a Channel Tunnel, these were firmly trounced.

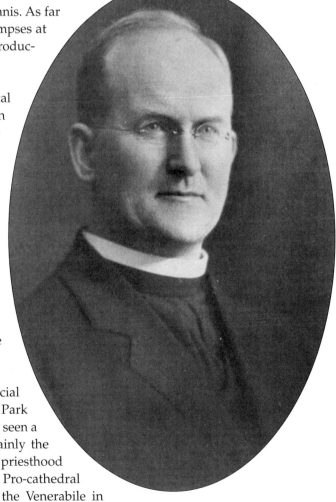

Despite hardships and threats to the established social order, things were felt to be satisfactory. At a Prior Park Association dinner, Br Roche claimed that he had 'never seen a finer Catholic spirit than amongst pupils today.' Certainly the great College tradition of producing candidates for the priesthood continued. Matthew Hayes was ordained priest in the Pro-cathedral in Bristol while Mervyn Alexander was ordained at the Venerabile in Rome. The College, it was announced on Speech Day, was 'trying to steer a middle course between out of date methods and modern superficial showiness'. Whatever the allure of unbridled 'newness', the Brothers were not about to 'cast aside their vast stores of experience'. Not everything in school work could be

Brother Roche.

The winning debating team of 1946. Brian Smith, Rae Carter and Dicky Buckley.

J.C. Murphy O'Connor.

'pleasant, entertaining or even amusing.' This somewhat stern Speech Day call for 'back to basics' was lightened by a young pianist, Cormac Murphy O'Connor, performing Beethoven and indeed winning a special prize for his piano playing. Like others of his family who went to Prior Park, he flourished also on the sports field particularly at rugby, and on the stage. In a production of *The Valiant* by Holsworthy Hall and Robert Middlemarsh, his performance as Josephine was highly commended. Particularly worthy of note, it was claimed, was the way he played with his fingers on his handbag, showing 'deep mental anguish.' Perhaps what brought most light and colour to these dark post-war years was the filming of *The Elusive Pimpernel* in the College grounds. The school magazine contains a charming picture of the actress Margaret Leighton, who starred as Lady Blakeney, standing on the Mansion steps surrounded by clearly smitten boys.

The filming of The Elusive Pimpernel *caused much interest among the boys.*

Warrant Officers and Non-Commissioned Officers, Prior Park College CCF, 1950. Back, standing: *L/c McAuly, L/cMahoney, L/cAuty, L/cBuller, Cpl Mucho, Cpl Bird, L/c Harding, Cpl Ball, Cpl Marenghi.* Centre, standing: *Cpl Kelly, Cpl Ford, Cpl Johns, Cpl Maher, Cpl Sampson, Cpl Lucas, Cpl Murphy, Cpl O'Keeffe, Cpl Mason.* Front, sitting: *Sgt Traynor, Sgt Taylor, CSM Savage, RSM Fowler, Brother Robinson, Brother O'Connell, CSM Garthwaite, CSM Mason, Sgt Davis, Sgt O'Connor.*

Members of the Combined Cadet Force.

Of course the international scene was darkened by the all too swift passage from the 'hot' war of '39-'45 to the so-called 'cold war'. Battle lines were now drawn up between the Soviet block and the West and guarded by the assurance of mutual destruction which could be delivered by a new generation of nuclear weapons. Prior Park was unusual amongst public schools in not as yet being involved in the Combined Cadet Force. But in 1949 the plunge was taken and the Ball Court, used by the local Home Guard as a rifle range during the Second World War, reverted to this role. The first parade of the cadet force showed all 'rather bashful and angular' and yet their drill was judged to be in good enough shape for them to parade at St John's Church for the Corpus Christi procession. At Speech Day Br Robinson was mildly apologetic about this development. He confessed that he was 'not an enthusiast for military organizations in schools' but it had to be faced that the world 'was in a very unsettled state. Grave dangers may arise threatening Christian civilization.' All no doubt would sleep more soundly with Sergeant Cormac Murphy O'Connor and his troops on parade.

The Corpus Christi procession of 1946.

Along with the slow painful rebuilding of Europe went some revival of confidence in religious institutions. The late forties and early fifties were a time of some growth for the Catholic Church. This was reflected in the life of Prior Park and its sons. Out in Nigeria former pupil Fr Frank Leahy baptized some 3500 adults and children in the course of one year. Solid advance was made in the religious life of the College under the leadership of its Chaplain Fr James Kelly who was also the parish priest for Combe Down. College and parish both made use of the Chapel. Bishop Lee had already urged Fr Kelly on to improve the quality of the school's liturgy. Fr Kelly needed little persuasion but the Brothers did. They came from that very Irish 'plain and basic' school of liturgy and shrank from fancy embellishments but the Chaplain managed to persuade the Brothers that English boys rather took to a bit of ceremonial and so a weekly High Mass was established.

Hockey XI, 1946.
B. Smith, J. O'Keefe, A. Seecombe, J. Adnett, J.D. Mason, H. McKenna, F. Lyons, P. Williams, J. Godwin, A.C. Bradford, P. Packwood and G. Walker.

The School Orchestra, 1952.

The Preparatory School at Cricklade.

When Fr Kelly was moved on to become the parish priest of St Alphege's in Bath, the school bade him a reluctant farewell. Tribute was in fact paid to the way in which he had furthered 'the liturgical spirit' and had impressed the community 'by his own quiet recollected air.' He was given as a parting present a 'fine wireless'. The mood of Catholic confidence found expression in the 1950 celebration of a Holy Year. For the College this included a trip to Rome, the highlight of which seems to have been attendance at an open-air performance of *Aida*. But perhaps the most significant sign of this Catholic self-confidence was the decision of the College as early as 1946 to establish a Preparatory School in north Wiltshire at Cricklade.

1951 began with a flurry of winter ills – gloomy skies, rain and a raging flu epidemic. The opening of Prior Park Parliament on 28 January brought some cheer. A rich variety of political opinion was represented – Conservatives, Communists, Socialists, Liberals, Sinn Fein, Fascists, and Welsh Nationalists were all there. But almost immediately the Conservatives were rent by division and a faction broke away to form the Rationalist Party. There is said to have been a 'rowdy evening' ending with the defeat of the Conservative Government. Locally spirits were raised by a visit to Filton to view that strange monstrous aeroplane, the Brabazon, which unlike the spirits could not be raised. It seemed spectacular in all but its ability to fly. But the biggest dose of good cheer was provided by the Festival of Britain, a rather deliberate and self-conscious government attempt to lift the spirits of a depressed post-war nation. Unexpectedly it seemed to work. On 29 June the Feast of SS Peter and Paul after Mass at 6.30 am, the College boarded a fleet of coaches to see the great exhibition and sights of London's South Bank.

John P. Ryan and Duchess, the Preparatory School mascot, standing outside Prior Park College.

The Lower V form in 1946.

The late forties and early fifties brought another flourishing of drama at Prior Park, this time under the direction of Hedley Goodall. *The Housemaster* by Ian Hay earned rave reviews in the *Bath and Wilts Chronicle and Herald*. *Arsenic and Old Lace* was greeted with similar enthusiasm while, of Kenneth Woollard's *Morning Departure*, the critic of the *Bristol Evening Post* declared; 'If I were awarding an Oscar for the season's best productions, it would unquestionably go to Hedley Goodall's presentation.' And so the critics seem to have fallen over each other in praise of these Prior Park productions. John Dighton's famous *The Happiest Days of your Life* had the *Bath Chronicle* critic writing that he had 'no hesitation in saying that of the many light comedies I have seen at the Theatre Royal during the past few months, only one or two have been as genuinely entertaining as this performance at Prior Park.' J.M. Barrie's *The Boy David* played to full houses. John Bogie gave a 'sturdy performance' as Saul while Patrick Ryan as David showed 'self-confidence, dramatic instinct, diction and intonation' which were all declared to be 'magnificent'. There were those at the school who, while granting that these productions were polished and slick, murmured that it was all a bit 'light-weight', that the plays chosen were too intellectually undemanding. However, the boys at Prior Park and at its sister College St Brendan's in Bristol, which also enjoyed the abilities of Hedley Goodall, seem to have appreciated what he had to offer. Mr Goodall, the critics said, 'must be weary of hearing his school productions in Bristol and Bath cited as shining examples to amateur societies, of how firm, disciplined, purposeful and imaginative direction can give inexperienced players an aura of accomplishment – yet the truth cannot be escaped.'

Hockey XI, 1948.

Standing: *G.L. Garthwaite, H.H. Hammond, J.G. Godwin, J. Mason, J.H. O'Keefe, F.J. Lyons.* Sitting: *F.A. Kelly, R.J. Carter, S.K. McCurley (Capt), P.A. Mullen, M Hanerton.*

"HOUSEMASTER"

CAST
(In order of their appearance)

Charles Donkin	...	Peter Scott
Bimbo Farringdon	...	Michael Starr
Victor Beamish	...	John Bogie
Frank Hastings	...	Charles Gomes
Ellen	...	Clifford Bura
Barbara Fane	...	John Richards
Button Fane	...	John Broughton
Matron	...	Anthony Corrigan
Rosemary Farringdon	...	Robin Holloway
Chris Farringdon	...	Michael Newling
Philip de Pourville	...	Brendan O'Driscoll
Flossie Nightingale	...	Malcom Drury
The Rev. Edmund Ovington		Alexander Motts
Sir Berkeley Nightingale	...	Cedric Hammond
Travers	...	Douglas Anderson
Pop	...	David Still
Old Crump	...	Roger Flower-Melling

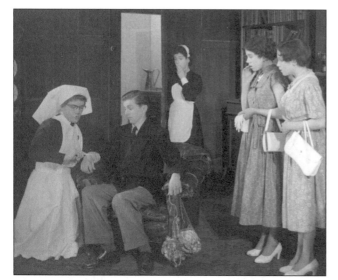

SCHOOL PLAY

'THE HAPPIEST DAYS OF YOUR LIFE'

A farcical Comedy by

JOHN DIGHTON

Cast

Tassell	.....	Terence Nichols
Rainbow	.....	Brian Chard
Billings	.....	Peter Sampson
Pond	.....	Jeremy Bisley
Miss Whitchurch	.....	Paul Wigmore
Miss Gossage	.....	James Peden
Hopcroft Minor	.....	Michael Starr
Barbara Cahoun	.....	Peter Scott
Joyce Harper	.....	Peter Hutchings
Rev. Edward Peck	.....	John Feeney
Mrs Peck	.....	Brendan O'Driscoll
Edgar Sowter	.....	Philip Withers
Mrs Sowter	.....	Nicholas Tranter

Pupils of St Swithin's and Hilary Hall: Gerald Jiggins, Edward Connolly, John Hammond, Geoffrey Cubitt, Anthony Tranter, Paul Doyle, Michael Blundell, Philip Greig.

The action of the play takes place in the Masters' Common Room at Hilary Hall School for Boys in Hampshire.

Act 1. The first day of the Summer Term. Afternoon.

Act 2. Saturday afternoon. Three weeks later.

Act 3. Two hours later.

The Setting Designed by	.....	Celia M. Lockett
Décor and Painting by	.....	Philip Massey
Assisted by Derek Plank, Geoffrey Barratt, Raymond Creese		
Set Built by	.....	Mr W. Gregory
Stage Manager	.....	William Packwood
Lighting under the direction of	.....	Peter Brown
Assisted by Jerome Smithson and Sean Anderson		
Properties	.....	Marcel Bartlett
The Play Produced by	.....	Hedley Goodall

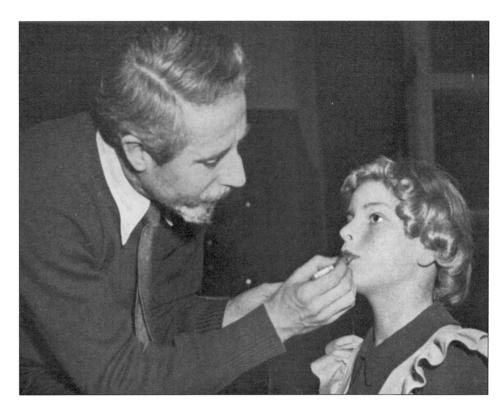

Hedley Goodall helping with make-up.

The Chapel of St Joseph which is in memory of Brother Roche.

In October 1951 the school was saddened by news of the death of Br Roche. Bishop Grimshaw, who presided at the funeral, spoke of 'a disciplinarian, even-tempered, very just, depending little upon corporal punishment, yet quite sure of being obeyed.' Roche was said to have been always ready to consider a 'good' excuse, which he firmly distinguished from a 'clever' one. The College was granted an afternoon off for singing so well at the Funeral Mass. Founded in the Brother's memory was the Roche Society dedicated to 'improving and maturing the thought and expression of the 6th Form by discussion of topics of real interest.'

In February of the following year the College along with the whole nation was shocked by another death, that of King George VI. After the news had broken 'the remainder of the day was carried on in a very subdued atmosphere'. Special prayers were said for the new Queen Elizabeth II at Compline and Benediction that Sunday. On 15 February a two-minute silence was observed during the late King's funeral. As a result of the King's death the England-Ireland rugby match was postponed. When it was finally played on 29 March, a number of boys from the school went to it. The weather was bitterly cold and so much snow had fallen that, on the return journey from Twickenham, boys had to alight from the coach to 'push it up one or two snow bound roads.' If the Lent term thus ended with snow, the summer term began with seemingly endless heavy rain. But that did not prevent John Bogie from taking 8 wickets for 7 runs, nor the College from celebrating the 150th Anniversary of the Founding of the Christian Brothers. After the Mass there was a whole gloriously free day. Indeed the College had a good deal to celebrate. With 245 pupils on the roll it had achieved record numbers and success was underlined by a vintage rugby season in 1954 with the first XV winning all its matches save the one against its sister College St Brendan's. And this was despite a flu epidemic which was so severe that the College had to break up a week early before the Christmas holidays.

The Corpus Christi procession of 1956.

1955 got off to another very cold start. In the Lent term pitches were frozen and hockey rarely played. The atmosphere of chill was added to by the showing of that classic of cold winds and wild wastes, the film *The Cruel Sea*. Winter seemed to drag on for so long, thus fulfilling the old saying, much beloved of Br Rice, that 'the cold is not out of the stone before St Patrick's Day'. In fact in 1955 the weather did not improve until July. On 21 May Lady Mountbatten visited the College and was greeted by a freak snow-storm. However, this did not deter pupils from being involved that month in the Bath Festival's dramatic reconstruction of the Battle of Trafalgar on the Recreation ground.

At Speech Day Br Beattie pondered on the relationship between the ethos of school and that of home. Were those same boys who were marched to Mass during the Term being similarly marched by their parents during the holidays? It was a question which could be called one hoping for the answer 'Yes' but knowing that the answer was often 'No'. Perhaps cracks were beginning to appear in the apparently solid edifice of Catholic practice. However Bishop Rudderham on the same occasion seemed to offer the young a more cheering message. 'You are not machines,' he declared, 'you are human boys and given the power to control and direct your own lives.' Yet before the said boys got the wrong idea and imagined that this might involve the 'power' to direct their steps from going to Mass, the Bishop added that they still needed to be shown how to direct and control their own lives. And that was what school was for!

Country dancing outside the Mansion.

But it was also for producing results as can been seen from the news of former pupils. Christopher Hocking won an Exhibition at Lincoln College, Oxford, leaving the school bereft of the Founder, President and sole member of its Archaeological Society. Other old boys were waking up to the delightful truth that life in Oxford meant being treated as 'a responsible individual' while the Cambridge correspondent took some pride in the fact that it was the Catholic Chaplain who was reckoned to be 'the best dressed man in Cambridge.' Anthony Levi was doing philosophy at the Jesuit College near Munich wrestling, he reported, with ' a very important but rather obscure book by Karl Rahner' which is at least some evidence that one of the sons of Prior Park was in touch with the up and coming new thinking in the Catholic Church. Out in Germany A.G. Watts marvelled at that nation's remarkable economic recovery making it rank 'as a power equivalent if not superior to England in industrial strength' while during the ill-fated Suez war another old boy Fred Cardozo found himself appointed as Senior Liaison Officer with the French. At this time too a glimpse is given of a further past as the death is recorded of Alfred John Dearlove who used to play cricket regularly for Gloucester with W.G. Grace.

Despite the success of old boys, Br Curran, the new President, was moved to express some concern at the 1956 Speech Day about A Level results. Of course, he

added, the school did not exist just for 'study and sound scholarship' but above all for 'religion and piety'. The trouble was that parents were increasingly unwilling to buy into the latter without some assurance of getting for their sons the former. The idea that Catholic schools could fill the gaps in educational excellence with piety seems to have been promoted at Speech Day in 1959 when it was breezily admitted that it was not 'characteristic of boys as a class to worry over much about their studies' but then, of course, education meant more than exams – 'religion and moral training formed the basis of the College's work.' This comforting doctrine was becoming harder to maintain. Yet to be fair, the College was making determined moves to broaden the curriculum and place a

Above: *The blessing of the new science building by Cardinal Godfrey and the Archbishop of Westminster.*

Right: *The new science block.*

greater emphasis on the sciences. By 1957 there were ambitious plans for a new science block which would be partly funded by a successful application to the Government's Industrial Fund for the Advancement of Scientific Education in Schools. So, despite Prior Park's suspicion of the Welfare State, it discovered that not everything was wrong with a bit of State support. The new science block was duly opened in July 1959 by Sir Graham Savage who called for the formation of eager young scientists who would 'make a new Industrial Revolution.' Cardinal Godfrey, who was also present, responded by blessing the building and urging pupils amidst all this newness not 'to forget the purpose of life – why we are made and what our destiny shall be.'

The Lady Chapel.

Certainly the Brothers made faith the centre of the College's life. The old pieties continued. During class God's presence was recalled throughout the day, as on the hour, when the clock struck, a Hail Mary would be recited. A Memorial Chapel was dedicated to that popular saint, to whom it was said the Cure D'Ars was particularly devoted, St Philomena. Unfortunately she was to become, like Oscar Wilde's Bunberry, 'quite exploded' when it was discovered that the inscription on which her very existence had depended, had been in fact sadly misread. But still reassuringly she stands in that side chapel a little dented now, her spear end broken but herself unbowed like some stately Queen Boadicea, become perhaps a role model for that later generation of girls who broke into this all-male world. There was a bit of a grumble in the fifties about the lack of volunteers to serve at the daily Mass, which seems to indicate some falling off of the number of communicants. Yet it was not all just doing the same old things – there was the introduction of an occasional 'Dialogue Mass', which, although still in Latin at this time, required greater congregational participation. A branch of the League of Christ the King was founded to encourage the study of particular real life situations and reflection on them in the light of faith, all to lead to the carrying out of some definite action. There was a further flourishing of sacred music. An up and coming young musician Chris de Souza played an active part as the Choral Society took on the challenging works of Rubbra and Holst.

A presentation to Chris d'Souza by Mr B.L. Bisgood KSG in 1956.

Boys hard at work in the new art room in 1955.

Hedley Goodall.

It was not only in religion that the new tried to mingle with the old. At a somewhat lower level Club Dixie and the Calypso Club were founded to satisfy a thirst for newness – although the College showed its hesitation about taking on such innovations by banishing them to the remaining old air raid shelters in the grounds. As old mingled with new, the Brothers continued to mix sacred with secular. After Benediction one night a new statue of Our Lady was blessed and installed on the Lady Altar in the Chapel and this was followed by a showing of the Hitchcock film *Dial M for Murder*.

On 11 February 1957, Br Rice was taken ill and died a few days later. His Requiem took place in the College Chapel on 19 February and was followed by burial in the Perrymead Cemetery. One of the educational experiences offered by schools run by religious orders was pupils' participation in the obsequies of departed monks, nuns and brothers thus enabling them to be confronted by the reality of death from which a more squeamish generation would shrink. There was usually offered the consolation of a half-day off to recover. Certainly Br Rice's demise does not seem to have overshadowed the 25 February dance with the girls from the Convent School, which was said to have 'gone with a swing.' The cricket that year was also of a high quality. When the MCC played the College, their team scored 241 for 4 declared, with the noted Somerset player Harold Gimblett getting 105, but the College responded strongly with 244 for no wickets. During the autumn Hedley Goodall presented as his farewell production *The Importance of Being Earnest* moving the *Bath Chronicle* to write that 'the acting was on a very high plain indeed' and 'the clarity of diction' simply 'wonderful'. Goodall's last stand had to compete with every school director's greatest enemy – illness, for it was in this autumn that the Asian flu epidemic struck. The school doctor Dr Leahy and the legendary school Nurse Keighery were stretched to the full with, at one time, 120 boys in bed in St Paul's and 60 in St Peter's.

12

NEGOTIATING A
STRANGE NEW WORLD

There seemed to be other dark clouds in the late 1950s. Sir David Kelly, a former Ambassador in Moscow, came to the College and shook his head at 'the tide of the movement towards egalitarianism', which he deemed to be 'an advance towards paganism'. Schools like Prior Park he declared to be in business to counter all this. But, while the imagination of the ex-Ambassador might have become fevered through his experience of the Soviet Union, there was other darkness around which was far from imagined. John Bryant, while on patrol in Cyprus, suffered multiple injuries from a terrorist bomb while J. Dieudonne was wounded in the Algerian conflict. The latter at least was able to return to his father's business in Paris – the House of Dior. And back at the school there was nothing imaginary in the pain caused by the death of thirteen-year-old Peter Austin O'Dowd carried off on 26 February by the 1959 Spring Term flu epidemic.

Br Curran, in his 1958 address on Speech Day, saw a further threat. 'The fact that the young were living in a period of great freedom was hardly to be celebrated' he declared. For this alleged freedom was pervaded by 'a spirit of independence and unfortunately a complete absence of supervision.' There was a need for 'strong and judicious supervision to be exercised by parents over their sons' various forms of recreation.' With this minatory tone the College prepared to greet the swinging sixties. A growing note of anxiety creeps into the voice, a fear that the firm hand of Catholic control will be lost over a new world with a new set of values. Yet on the same Speech Day, Patrick McGrath, lecturer in history at Bristol University and noted Tudor scholar, viewed the challenge of this new world with some confidence. There was, he declared, a dangerous tendency of Catholics 'to look in on ourselves instead of outwards upon the world.' Faith, he insisted, needed to 'grow up' to become mature faith. Catholic schools should be not only 'pious schools' but 'good schools' as well, providing quality education. He ended his speech by declaring that 'although Prior Park seems to me to be in every way an admirable institution, I would not dream of sending my own children to it nor, for that matter, would Prior Park dream of accepting them, unless by some curious twist of fortune, it became a girls' school, but this I imagine is unlikely to happen!' It is pleasing to record that the unlikely did happen, fortune duly twisted and Prior Park became such that Dr McGrath lived to see his daughter Katrina become

Brother Curran.

Pope Pius XII who died in 1958.

a distinguished student at the College. However at the time his comment may have raised a good laugh but it also touched on a raw nerve for suggestions were beginning to fly around that Prior Park might have to broaden its intake. The Bishop himself believed that it should take on day-boys and others even wondered about an advance into co-education. The Brothers were resolute in resisting all such blandishments. Back in 1946 Canon Hackett, the parish priest of St John's in Bath, had written to Br Odo MacNamara, the Provincial of the English province of the Christian Brothers, commending the inclusion of day boys but had received a pretty bleak reply. 'I believe' wrote Br Odo 'that the admission of day-pupils of the type contemplated would (a) lower the status of the College; (b) cause grave practical inconvenience in the matter of holidays, half-holidays, mid-day meals, etc; (c) increase the risk of infection; (d) above all, cause many boarders to be withdrawn.' The Provincial did not make clear whether the feared 'infection' was of a physical or moral nature.

But, whether they liked it or not, change of an even more far-reaching nature was on the way. On Sunday 9 October 1958 Pope Pius XII died and within a short while the College of Cardinals had elected as his successor the elderly Patriarch of Venice Angelo Giuseppe Roncalli to become Pope John XXIII. It was generally thought that he would be a 'caretaker' pope; at his age content to allow church life to go quietly on. As the College sat back to enjoy his Coronation Mass, that is no doubt what the Brothers expected from the new Pope. But this was the man who wrote in his diary on the day of Pius XII's death: 'we are not on earth as museum-keepers, but to cultivate a flourishing garden of life and to prepare for a glorious future.' As it turned out the old man was a Pope who dared not only to look forward but also to look outward on a world which was not to be seen as the Church's enemy but as that to which it is sent to love and serve. What the boys of Prior Park expected from the Pope is not recorded but what is recorded, is that three days after the Coronation Mass, they were able to declare the dance with the Convent girls 'the best so far'.

But then came, as it were signs from heaven. In April of the following year, in the early hours of the morning, a digger struck the water main at the top of Ralph Allen Drive sending a cascade past the teaching block, turning the steps into a veritable Niagara, and on down the bank to flood the downstairs of St Paul's. As pyjama-clad Brothers leapt to the rescue, boys regretted that there was no *Bath Chronicle* photographer at hand to record the event. In November of the following year, the Geography Society listened to a talk on how the flooding problems of Bath, at that time many and frequent, were to be solved and, as if to illustrate the need for this, on 17 November the Convent School was flooded. That led to another flood – that of boys eagerly volunteering to go to the girls' rescue.

So it is said the 1960s swept over post-war English Society. It was in truth an unstoppable flood, an era of upheaval. There is a note of unease in Br Beattie's voice on Speech Day as he asks rhetorically whether Pop music is 'the best life has to offer'. Parents should beware, he counselled, of the possible ill effects of 'prolonged sessions' of such listening. But he reassured his audience that he did not 'expect this epidemic to become a chronic condition'. Out at Cricklade the parish priest of Winchester shook his head over 'the sickness of contemporary society' and warned the prep school of the dangers of 'adolescent revolt.' While the new Pope was busy throwing open the windows of the Vatican, there was still more than a little anxious Catholic manning of the barricades.

The clear up operation begins, April 1959.

The sixties turbulence in truth came at a sensitive time for the College. Not only was there a need to expand facilities to cope with increasing parental demands but also the nature of the buildings, which the school had inherited, meant that they required constant attention. Like other buildings in Bath they might be visually glorious but could also hide some jerry-building behind the scenes. The Brothers were conscious of a mounting backlog of work to be done and of the financial implications of carrying this out. Speech Days begin to contain expressions of gratitude to a 'patient Bank Manager'. And then to add to the worries, along came the introduction of Selective Employment Tax. All this meant that, at a crucial moment, which called out for both urgent repair and expansion of facilities, there had in fact to be a cut-back in the building programme.

But the Brothers made the best of things. After all not everything was doom and gloom. A school inspection left the College feeling 'that we were going in the right direction.' Which is more than can be said of the Chief of the Imperial General Staff, Sir Francis Festing who came to inspect the CCF in July 1960. He managed to arrive at the Top Gate rather than at the Mansion where the party of VIPs were waiting to greet him. The troops collected by this Top Gate on the cricket field had just endured a heavy shower of rain and were worrying whether the new bass drum would suffer from this exposure. But now it was like the Day of the Lord – there when they were not expecting him was suddenly the Inspecting General.

Inspection of the CCF in 1960.

Quick action by the senior Under-Officer brought the parade to attention, the band played and the general salute was given. Meanwhile a runner had been dispatched to the Mansion to collect the President and other VIPs. Thus a shame-faced perspiring party arrived on the field to find everything in full swing.

Musically the College was also in full swing. A demanding concert of twentieth century choral work on 'The Three Persons of the Trinity' was performed. This included music by Elgar, Rubbra and Vaughan Williams. A full orchestra accompanied the singing with Chris de Souza leading the second violins. The *Bath Chronicle* wrote of 'the exquisite singing' to be heard. Members of the elite choir,

The Artillery Section of the CCF in 1966.

The Artillery Section of the CCF in 1968.

Schola, sang the Corpus Christi Mass on BBC radio. But there were also achievements athletic as well as aesthetic. The sixties indeed saw some vintage years of Prior Park rugby. In 1966 the 1st XV played seventeen games and won eleven of them. Along with this went some burgeoning of school societies. The Scientific Society showed to its members a film on 'What goes into a Blast Furnace' and had a lecture on 'The Refining of Oil'. A lot was going well and Br Beattie was justified in talking of 'quiet development'.

Although, with the retirement of Hedley Goodall, there was a temporary decline in the College's drama, it could continue to take satisfaction in those whom it had given to the world of theatre. J. Bisley won a contract with the BBC to pioneer a new Shakespeare series 'An Age of Kings'. Chris de Souza launched his career in opera whilst still a student at Bristol University where his production and designs for Gluck's *Iphegenia in Aulis* won high acclaim from critics in both the *Daily Telegraph* and the *Sunday Times*. Whilst at Prior Park, the young Cameron Mackintosh had dreamed dreams of producing plays and presenting them at the Bristol Hippodrome. He had come to Prior Park expecting to experience the skills of Hedley Goodall but now the star had fled which probably explains why there is little evidence that Mackintosh

Cadet Corporal B Haddrell receives the Atlantic Trophy from Group Captain A Reece.

himself engaged much in the drama scene at the school. Perhaps his sights were set a little higher for he was either granted or had grabbed the freedom to go down to Bath to be involved in the highly prestigious Octagon Theatre in Milsom Street. He himself puts the firing of his ambition down to being dragged to the Theatre Royal in Bristol to see Julian Slade's famous cult fifties musical, *Salad Days*. From Prior Park he went on to Drama School and then to be an Assistant Stage Manager for Lionel Bart's new musical *Oliver*. By the age of twenty-one he was one half of the team presenting *Little Women* at that goal of his, the Bristol Hippodrome. By the age of twenty-three Cameron Mackintosh was into his 10th production.

A quick glance at the *Prior Park Association News* shows other old boys achieving great things in an impressive variety of jobs. There is Peter Levi producing the first volume of his poetry while teaching archaeology in Oxford. Hugh Scully at the BBC was already doing a weekly feature on antiques. John Walsh had now become Director of the famous National Spinal Injury Unit at Stoke Mandeville while, out in California, Philip Ryan was practising as a Brain Surgeon and, in Southern Rhodesia, Alec Graham was a cardiac surgeon. With William Spencer becoming a fellow of Sydney Sussex College in Cambridge and Peter Ashworth manager of a brewery in New Guinea, it could be said that the College was delivering a wide range of goods. Old Boys were to gather for their dinner in London with their guest of honour Nurse Maira Keighery to celebrate her twenty-five years service at Prior Park. Her presence made it possible for other ladies to be present.

Sister M.E. Keighery at her Silver Jubilee celebration.

Meanwhile in Rome the old Pope was plotting new things. He was poised to do what had not been done since 1870, call a great general Council of the Catholic Church. On 11 October 1962 he opened what is called the Second Vatican Council,

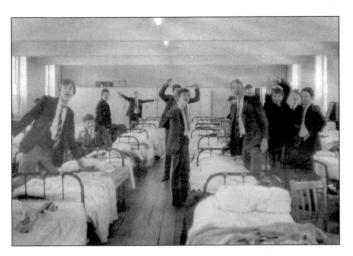

A dormitory in 1960. Many boys shared one room with only a bed, chair and locker each. There was little room for privacy.

Supplementing the daily rations.

which was to be arguably the most important religious event of the twentieth century. It offered the possibility of an end to an era of siege mentality for Roman Catholics, which had stretched, from the Reformation through the French Revolution to the dawning of secular societies. That mentality is summed up in Pio Nono's minatory 'Syllabus of Errors', which managed to condemn almost anything, which had about it the whiff of modernity. But Pope John XXIII opened his council with a summons 'not merely to hoard this precious treasure' (of the Gospel) 'but to give ourselves eagerly and without fear to the task that the present age demands of us.' It has to be said that the sound of opening windows was somewhat muted at Prior Park. While this extraordinary event was going on and despite the fact that their near neighbour, Abbot Christopher Butler of Downside, was deeply involved in it all and highly articulate about it, there is little evidence that either staff or pupils at Prior Park were aware of what was going on. There is though some apprehension that 'coming changes in the Liturgy may diminish the activities of Schola' and some irritation with it all.

The Brothers had produced a style of Catholic life which emphasised solid, if rather dull, religious practice which yet produced solid results in good practical Christian living. Plain and basic was the diet and there was clearly much merit in it. There could not be too much wrong with the quiet unostentatious piety cultivated by the Brothers which could produce men like C.K. Neville Davie, a chartered accountant who went daily to Mass in the City of London but who died at the early age of thirty-six ministered to by his fellow Prior Park old boy, the Franciscan Fr Jackie Ward. Religious changes which upset such established patterns of devotion are never an unqualified good and yet, if John Henry Newman were right that faith is a great living stream carrying the gospel through differing ages and cultures, then change there had to be. To live is indeed to change. There were pupils like Brian Smith who, while acknowledging that they were taught ' all the tenets of the Roman Catholic faith', admits that he left Prior Park ' a highly bigoted Roman Catholic' which he came to see was not 'a good basis for working and living' not only with other Christians but also those of other religions. He regretted the narrowness of it all and lived to welcome the wider more generous vision of Vatican 2.

Fr Langford, the new parish priest, busily engaged in overseeing the building of the Church of SS Peter and Paul in Combe Down, yet found time to come to the College to introduce a twentieth century Folk Mass. Boys, who tend to be very conservative, were not sure what to make of it. But it certainly stirred up some heated discussion. Christopher Hollis, for some years MP for Devizes and a Governor of the College, perhaps caught the mood of the times as he guided the school to confront the delicate issue of the relationship of the Vatican, during the reign of Pius XII, with the Jewish people. Professor Whalley, on Speech Day 1964, embraced the Council's call for change, welcomed the Catholic Church's new involvement in the search for unity amongst Christians, and called for a process of continuing re-education both secular and sacred. G.J. Alston claimed that 'loyalty to the Church' now needed to be more critical and intelligent and, perhaps somewhat prematurely, claimed that the hierarchy was waking up to the need for a real and full partnership with the laity. In a similar vein, Dick Farrell, out in

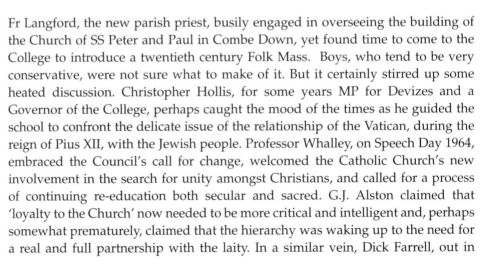

Ottawa, wrote enthusiastically of the 'fresh dynamic Catholic life' he found in Canada, especially with its emphasis on 'lay participation.' So perhaps in these ways something of the message of the Council was getting through to Prior Park.

One of the eventual effects of the Council in the College's life can be seen in a turning outward from the small world of a boarding school to take seriously the needs of the neighbourhood in which it was set. Pupils began to be involved in such things as the 'Old Folks Club' in Combe Down, in schemes for the painting and decorating of pensioners' houses and working in their gardens. Boys from Prior Park were to join with girls from Bath High School in surveying facilities for the disabled in the hotels and restaurants of the city. Br Hooper publicly applauded 'the compassion of the young of today'. He said that they were 'far more conscious of the needs of others than older generations'. They knew how to give generously of themselves.

It seems that it took until the next decade for the spirit of the sixties to strike the Governors. In 1970, with a rush of blood to the head, they voted to allow 6th Form boys, over the age of sixteen, to smoke. To avail themselves of this privilege they had to have the written permission of their parents and it was instructed that posters be displayed advertising the risk of cancer. From the vantage point of the risk-sensitive twenty-first century, this would seem to be about the last freedom a Governing body would bestow and certainly later generations of school authorities had to work hard to reverse this decision. But, just as the lads were (officially) lighting up, the 1971 power workers' strike was plunging the College into darkness. There were constant power cuts, which led to evening study by candlelight and, rather more romantically, the annual dance with the Convent girls to be lit in the same way.

Brother Hooper.

In June 1971 there came the news of the death of Br Burke out in Ireland where he had retired after forty-six years of service to the College. 'Outside God' Denis Gilmer wrote 'he had but one love, Prior Park.' Memories came flooding back of this godly stalwart – of the one who, even then at a considerable age, insisted on taking his turn at fire-watching during the war – of the man who calmly continued at his correspondence during the great raid and who only dropped his pen when the bomb fell outside his study, and who was discovered still at his desk uninjured amidst the rubble of St Paul's – of the zealous rugby supporter standing on the touchlines shouting 'Feet! Feet! Feet! – On Prior!'. He was something of an early and instinctive PR expert for it was he who had enticed the Australian Prime Minister, during the Coronation Year, to Prior Park and who carefully cultivated old Queen Mary and encouraged her many visits. They said that, as he got older, he harped on somewhat tediously about the 'great days of old'. But that is what all old men tend to do and if he was sometimes, as they claimed, 'irritating', he was always 'loveable'.

There were deaths of other notables around this time. Br Cowley died in 1972 as did Mr Gregory who had been the college maintenance man since 1919 and who

A house photograph c 1970.

The Murphy O'Connor family.

left as a permanent memorial of his skills, much of the wood panelling in St Paul's. Norah Hodges was the honoured guest at a dinner to mark her retirement after fifty years of service to the music of Prior Park but she died very soon after this. The school was shocked by the sudden death in 1976 of James Guest the senior history master. Then amongst old boys, there was the death of Sir Francis Walshe, the distinguished neurologist who had won a reputation for boldly challenging accepted medical dogma with criticisms, which were said to have been 'rapier like in their penetration and their wit.' His conversation, they said, was always adorned 'by Celtic idiom and a sense of ridicule.' Sir Wulstan Dixie also died. He was a rather different product of the College. The Thirteenth Baronet of Market Bosworth who sported 'a luxurious handle-bar moustache', drove powerful sports cars and, despite of or because of, his 'unmistakeable stutter' was held to be a great 'ladies' man', was judged to have stepped straight out of a P.G. Wodehouse novel. And then tragically and heroically, there died John Clements at the age of twenty-two in an Italian hotel fire after he had saved the lives of some 21 children. For this he was awarded posthumously the George Cross.

Prior Park Association News showed how old boys were living as well as dying. Cormac Murphy O'Connor who had become Rector of the English College in Rome in 1971 did not stay there long, for a few years later he was to become Bishop of Arundel and

Brighton. Numerous members of his family had passed through Prior Park. With three eminent clerics and a rugby international, it was said that the family effected 'a happy balance between sacred and secular'. Mervyn Alexander was appointed auxiliary Bishop to Bishop Rudderham who was in failing health and whom he succeeded as Bishop of Clifton in 1974. The College was continuing to send out men to heal bodies as well as souls. Anthony Finnegan served as a GP in Oxford, becoming medical officer for St Hugh's College, fathered six children and played chess for the county. Michael Brotherton was elected the Conservative MP for Louth in Lincolnshire and still the College went on making a contribution to the world of the arts and the theatre. Chris de Souza was by now producing operas at Sadlers Wells; David Whitaker was composing music for films, notably for *Dr Jekyll and Sister Hyde*. The stream of Cameron Mackintosh productions continued to flow. He achieved his tenth production *Anything Goes* by the time he was twenty-three, and soon he was to bring *My Fair Lady* and *Godspell* to Bristol. Anthony Essen-Lopresti became head of documentaries for Yorkshire TV and produced a notable 26-episode programme on 'The Great War'. Anthony Brannon, after being Tour Manager for the singer Tom Jones, disappeared to Bermuda to be in charge of 'The Forty Thieves' Club.'

Meanwhile the College, which had launched these men into this impressive variety of careers, seemed to be going quite well. Some improvements were made to facilities. An all-weather pitch was created to serve the needs of hockey players and a new cricket pavilion was built in memory of Br Burke. With the future international John Palmer playing for the 1st XV, rugby had two successful years. The school drama made something of a come-back. After an attempt by Sidney Ash to produce a comedy by Plautus had failed to take off, Pat McMahon managed in 1970 to bring a production of Willis Hall's *The Long, the Tall and the Short* to fruition. The following year began a period of successful co-operation between Prior Park and the Convent School in a series of productions under the leadership of Helen McFarlane from the girls' school with the assistance of Pat and Maureen McMahon and Tony Ryan for the home side. *Pride and Prejudice*, *The Italian Straw*

Sidney and Mary Ash with Wilfrid de Freitas and Peter Hilton.

Cricket XI, 1951
Standing: *G.M. Bowder, P.S. Farinha, D.S. Bogie, M.J. Birch, S.B. Farinha, B.L. Camps-Campins, W.N. Patterson.* Sitting: *J.H. Mahoney, W.L. Mason, D.J. McAuley (Capt), P. Brown, J.R.A. Scott-Oldfield.*

Hat and *Pygmalion* – all showed that there was life still in the drama. And there were also the quieter achievements. John Weston began his remarkable years of service to the College with his Radio Club while, out in the community, volunteer boys continued to collect firewood, do gardening and some painting and decorating for pensioners and joined in the national winter weather scheme which involved visiting lonely elderly people.

With all this and with numbers remaining buoyant, the College could, with some confidence, celebrate in September 1974 the fiftieth Anniversary of the Christian Brothers' re-opening of Prior Park. Archbishop Dwyer of Birmingham presided at the Mass with Bishop Mervyn Alexander. There were seven other concelebrating old boy priests providing a timely reminder that, during this period, the College had given some 40 priests to the Church. A Five Part Byrd Mass was sung and the local press commented on 'the glorious sound of masculine voices proclaiming their faith in the Credo in Latin.' The Archbishop also gave his blessing in Latin – an ending to the Mass, which was followed by a trumpet fanfare. At the speeches, which followed the Mass, Fergus Lyons recalled, with some wit and indeed irreverence, the history of a project, which had 'started as a postman's dream to become a Bishop's nightmare.' The mild levity of this speech while entertaining most of his audience caused some displeasure amongst the Brothers.

THE FLICKERING PHOENIX

Just as the lights went out at the beginning of the decade so there is evidence that towards its end there was some faltering, flickering and failing. At Speech Day there is shaking of the head at the problem of 'growing religious illiteracy', while the 5th Form is summoned to a 'greater sense of urgency and purpose' and the prefects called upon to give a 'better lead'. Br Power had to admit that exam results were not so good. Freedom was being abused and there was 'slacking where there should be studying'. In fact a Junior Drones Club had been established for such slackers involving detention on Sunday afternoons. All this was stern stuff for such a public event as a Speech Day which is not normally thought to be the occasion for the washing of dirty linen. But in the late seventies there are murmurings of indiscipline and a loss of control. Senior boys were said to spend weekday evenings down in Bath, returning for a Roll Call at 9pm before plunging back into the fleshpots until the early hours of the mornings. Such a hectic pace of social life seems to have had an impact on scholarly life. It is alleged that this nightlife led to senior boys often taking a leisurely lie-in in the mornings.

An aerial photograph of the College, c1960.

Ken Russell, filming at Prior Park. Reproduced by kind permission of the *Bath Chronicle*.

The College was faced with two big problems. In company with other religious orders at this time, the Christian Brothers were experiencing a sharp decline in vocations. There were now fewer Brothers to man their schools. At the same time the Second Vatican Council had made their Order, like others, review their mission, to ask critically whether what they were doing was what they had been founded to do. In some of the most deprived areas of the North West and North East of England, the Brothers were clearly following in the footsteps of Edmund Rice, but was running a public school in the more affluent West Country really what they were meant to be doing? Such questionings, though necessary, do not make for confident advance. Increasingly there were gaps to be filled in the teaching staff and, over recent years, the Brothers were employing more lay teachers. This change was to begin with both slow and reluctant. These new members of staff were always called 'the visiting staff' so were positively encouraged to be '9 – 5' teachers with no involvement in the wider life of the school. The running of

Patrick Ferreira receives an award.

Prior Park First XV lineout.

At study.

a boarding school, with all those evening and long weekend duties, was the sole responsibility of that dwindling red line of Brothers. When Sidney Ash joined the staff in 1946, he was the only full-time lay member of staff. Of course things could not remain this way. The numbers of lay staff grew and they began to be slipped into other 'extra-mural' activities – the refereeing of sports, involvement in the drama and so on. Yet they continued to be called 'the visiting staff'. Sidney Ash recalled how the Brothers were still reluctant to involve them in duties outside the classroom. When, in some emergency, he was asked to take an evening prep, he was anxiously asked whether he could 'manage it'. One suspects that it was the failure to overcome this staff division that both laid intolerable burdens on the remaining Brothers and led to an unacceptable delegation of responsibility to inadequate prefects. No wonder discipline was strained and control lost.

The second problem which the College faced was an old and familiar one – money. Resources were short; financial demands were great, and book-keeping does not seem to have been one of the Brothers' charisms. The feeling was beginning to be expressed quite openly that the 'continued existence of Prior Park was something of a miracle.' By now the history of the College should have shown that Bishop Baines's total trust in 'Divine Providence' was not quite enough. Not even the most Catholic of schools can live by miracle alone. So it was considered that the Jubilee celebrations provided an opportunity for an appeal for funds to be launched. It seems to have had but modest success.

Significantly at this point Br Power stood down as President and went on sabbatical leave. The strain for the leadership was becoming clearly too great. His place was taken by Br Miller and the change was, in fact, warmly welcomed by the staff. They knew that here was someone who saw clearly both that change was needed and where it was needed and so they looked forward to a time of bustling, if uncomfortable, activity. But is never came. Nothing happened. If anything there was increased inactivity. Why, they asked, were not things being done that they all knew Br Miller believed should be done? What they did not know was that their new leader was sitting on a deadly paralysing secret. The Phoenix was once more drooping.

THROUGH TEMPEST AND FIRE INTO THE FUTURE

O n 7 March 1980, Br Miller gathered the staff to announce that the Christian Brothers were to be withdrawn from Prior Park in July of the following year. Br Miller had known this for some time but had had to keep this information to himself while highly discreet feelers had been put out to other religious orders to see if they were interested in taking over the school. None were, for all religious were in the same boat as the Brothers – a shortage of vocations combined with a critical scrutiny of their mission. The very future of the College was once again threatened.

Happily Br Miller's news came out just as old boys were gathering for a Prior Park Association weekend. It was over the course of that weekend that the fight to save the College was launched. The moment, it was said, 'found the man', John Bogie, who was acclaimed to have been 'the driving force behind Prior Park's salvation.' But there were many others ready and willing to follow his lead. Governors, old boys and lay staff came together to set up an Action Committee which consisted

The Christian Brothers' farewell dinner, including wives of lay staff.

of Fergus Lyons, Chris Glover, Ferdi Sanchez, Jim Coelho, Mostyn Thomas, Sidney Ash and Pat McMahon. John Bogie was appointed clerk to the committee and a 'fighting fund' was established. It was clear that the future of the College was going to be under lay leadership and this was emphasised in the appointment of Trustees. Although Mervyn Alexander, Bishop of Clifton, took his rightful place amongst them and was joined by other clerics, including that stalwart of Old Boys, Bishop Cormac of Arundel and Brighton and, as a gesture of reconciliation with the College's Benedictine roots, Abbot Victor Farwell OSB, there was a notable 'lay' weighting: Miles, Duke of Norfolk, Norman St John Stevas, Lord Clifford of Chudleigh, and the then local Member of Parliament, Chris Patten. The steely determination of old boys and the decisive action taken meant that on the 28 May Speech Day John Bogie was able to announce, to prolonged and enthusiastic applause, that the College had a future.

For Br Miller this Speech Day was a bitter-sweet occasion. He expressed the regrets of the Christian Brothers at having to take this action. He knew what the popular image of a typical Brother was, 'a raw-boned Irishman clutching a catechism in one hand and wielding a strap in the other'. But what they had struggled to do was to form 'a solid practical Christianity and a happy blend of strictness and flexibility, of dignity and informality.' In these blends Br Miller was trying to express a quite deliberately chosen style of community life which sought to be a bit different from the image of a typical 'public school'. It is a style which, as we shall see, mattered intensely to pupils, and whose loss they greatly feared. However the last President of Prior Park was able also to celebrate the sweetness of the occasion as he paid handsome tribute to the Action Committee and the staff. The College was to have a future and to those who asked whether it would 'be the same when the Brothers left', he was able to point in answer to the stated intention of the Staff and Trustees 'to maintain the spirit' of the place.

Then, turning to other events of the year, Br Miller could now openly admit that bold new actions had been inhibited by the Congregation's decision. Plans to expand the drama and music departments had thus been shelved. All in all it had been a 'bread and butter' sort of year but he insisted, surely 'good' bread and butter. The school rugby had been successful with the 1st XV winning eight of its matches and losing only three. In all this Damian Cronin, the future Scottish international, who was developing 'into a player of some distinction', had played an effective part. The school magazine commended his jumping in the lineout but added that he 'has still a lot to lean about physical confrontation.' As a final sign of hope for the future Br Miller was able to announce that the punitive Drones Club for idle scholars had been disbanded for lack of members.

If Prior Park had a future it would need a new Joshua to lead it into that Promised Land. An advertisement was placed for a lay Head Teacher. Patrick Tobin's Aunt Koo spotted it and directed her nephew's attention to it. Although, at that time, Head of History at Tonbridge School, he was actually in Australia on a teaching exchange. When he took advice about the advisability of applying for this job, he received some fairly mixed messages. There were colleagues who thought the whole idea rather 'rum', his son wondered whether his father 'was ready to be a headmaster' and perhaps the best consolation came from a friend, who pointed out that, if a school closes, 'they always need the Headmaster to stay on for a few years afterwards to clear up the mess.' However Patrick Tobin took the plunge, applied for the job, came for interview and was appointed with the daunting task of launching the new regime in the autumn of 1981

Patrick Tobin.

The year between the announcement of the Brothers' departure and the beginning of the new order was not an easy one. A special Open Day was held in March 1981 to lay before parents something of Patrick Tobin's dream for the revived school. It was, he declared, 'a unique opportunity to build an Independent Catholic school, in tune with the spirit of the Church today, on the basis of the dedication and commitment left by the Christian Brothers.' Assurance was given of continuity of purpose but also of a future, which, he promised, would be 'an exciting and stimulating experience.' It was going to prove certainly all of that. The past could not be forgotten. How could it be with the death of Kitty Perry, one of the Irish girls who had come to work at Prior Park? Kitty had arrived as a teenager, inhabited the none-too-salubrious attics of the Mansion, until she got married and brought up her family in Combe Down. All these years she continued to serve the College, making sure that, as she arrived and left, she paid a visit to the Blessed Sacrament. On her death she was hailed as 'the saint of Combe Down'. So at Speech Day that year, the last under the Christian Brothers, there was much of the past to celebrate and be thankful for. Br Miller declared that 'they would prefer to retire without a fanfare of trumpets certainly not of their own blowing' but admitted that the 'pain of parting was eased by the promise of continuation'.

Just before the autumn term launching of the new order, Bishop Cormac presided over a Staff Colloquium at which he commended and promoted the virtue of 'stickability'. The virtue was shrewdly chosen, as it would indeed be needed in

The Governing Body of 1981. Mr C.P.E. Colombotti, Chris Glover, Adrian Snow, Dom Raphael Appleby, Rear Admiral John Robertson, John Leay, Col Ronnie Dowden, Tony Sutton, Tony Mason, Chris Glover, Denis Gilmer, Patrick Tobin, Fergus Lyons, John Bogie, Dr Finola Roche, Mervyn Scott.

large doses over the next few years. Patrick Tobin of course inherited a number of the old lay staff, Sidney Ash, Pat McMahon, Tony Ryan, Brian Bane, Cy Symonds, Denis Clarke, John Moran, Tony O'Sullivan amongst them, but there were new appointments to be made. Richard Wells came from the Wildlife Trust at Slimbridge to teach biology and Andrew Mock from the ranks of the BBC Northern Singers to be Director of Music. Then there was the important task of appointing Housemasters to replace the Brothers who had always jealously guarded this role for themselves. Tobin was looking for married men who, with wives and families would create something new, a family atmosphere in the houses. So John and Elizabeth Moran moved into St Peter's and a newcomer Dr Peter Walshe with his wife Ann, took over St Paul's. Walshe was a man of the left, a supporter of Liberation Theology, but combined this with reassuring Oxford Blues in both hockey and cricket.

Two other vital appointments were made. Eileen McPeake was enticed from Berkhamsted School to be the School Matron and Father Paul Edwards, a priest of

Girls Hockey 1st XI, 1986

Back row: *Mr B. Bane, E. Jeffery, L. Browning, Z. Herrero, T. Hart, C. Nash, L. O'Flaherty, Mr A.W. O'Sullivan.* Front row: *M. Wood, J. Hall, S. Angelo-Sparling (Capt), R. Eke, S. Miles, G. Davies.*

The First XI Cricket Team of 1993

Back row: *T. Lamb, L. Dokic, A. Smith, A. Kennedy, I. Okoli, Mr D. Holland (coach).* Front row: *P. Beatty, C. O'Brian, P. Bennett (Capt), C. Hathoway, M. Madden.*

2nd XV Rugby 1999

Back: *A. Hardy, H. Reynolds, K. Raeisi, A. Lee.* Middle: *I. Clarke, B. Davies, S. Wallace, H. Woloszynski, A. Dicorato, V. Hackshaw, Mr Davies.* Front: *O. Templeton, C. Heffer, P. Brown, R. Hanbury (Capt), K. Mulemba, R. Upton.*

Bath Seven-A-Side Champions 1974

N. Wrightman (Capt), receiving the Colts Trophy from Mr George Brown, President of Bath Rugby Club. Others left to right: G.D. Hull, M.S. Hickey, M.H. Baker, M.G. Limpert-Peers, J.A. Palmer, S.C. Spencer.

1st Tennis Squad 2002

Back: *A. Creed, L. Sturgess, Mr G. D. Pruett.* Front: *P. Reed, M. Delaney, F. Whitwell (Capt),*
T. Jones, M. Davis.

Under 14 B Hockey 2003

Back: *H. Hall.* Middle: *H. Smith, J. Swannell, L. Nadin, S. Johnson, M. Lam, O. Gilmour.* Front:
C. Perkins, C. Johnson, T. Maxwell (Capt), J. P. Indoe, H. Davies.

the Diocese of Arundel and Brighton, was allowed by his Bishop to become Chaplain. Fr Paul had a heart condition judged sufficiently severe to prevent him from being in charge of a parish but that heart must have been sorely tested in his new post for he put every bit of it into the task. Sporting a white beard and looking like a cross between Father Christmas and one of the dwarves in Snow White, Paul Edwards was warm, witty and very shrewd. He had come to the priesthood by a hard route. Brought up in Shanghai he spent two and a half years in a Japanese internment camp and, after the war, he had fifteen years working as an account-ant before becoming a priest. Here was a mature man then who, with his dog Dona and an early passion for computers, easily won the hearts of both pupils and staff. John Bogie, having headed up the rescue operation, was now appointed the Head of the Preparatory School at Cricklade. He was to make a further lasting contribution to the new order by ensuring the appointments of George Jenkins, an ex-army NCO, as the Clerk of Works, Susie Holmes as the Headmaster's PA, and Jane Floyd to undertake the task of managing the introduction of the new school uniform.

This was to prove a powerful team but it was going to need firm leadership and hard work to weld such a variety of talent together. Inevitably some of the 'old guard' on the staff were not sure how to take all this newness. It really did mean a revolution in their way of working. Used to being treated as the 'visiting staff' and not greatly encouraged to be involved in the running of the school, they found that all this had to change. Now they were to be all up to their necks in that school life. The pace was hectic and some found the hands-on Patrick Tobin a driving force hard to keep up with. Autumn 1981 saw a veritable explosion of activity – an Open Day to reassure a sceptical public that Prior Park was still in business, the negotiation of a difficult Old Boys' Reunion at which significantly the older ones were more positive about the new regime than were the younger, a triumphantly successful carol service organized by Andrew Mock, and finally a great Palladian Ball at which not all pupil behaviour was at its best. Tobin's colleagues were exhausted. Staff-meetings had been lengthier and meetings for Housemasters often advanced well into the night.

But it was all necessary. The College really was fighting for survival. The summer exam results were even more dreadful than had been feared. Instead of Tobin inheriting the 260 pupils, there were only 232. And then there was an 'old guard' amongst the boys. They frankly and openly mourned the loss of the Brothers. They were, as all schoolboys are, suspicious of 'newness' and resistant to attempts to bring a clearer order and discipline to the community. They complained that, instead of the old informality, an attempt was being made to turn their beloved Prior Park into Eton. The new regime was 'draconian' in its stripping away of Sixth Form privileges, its assault on smoking and its control of 'lights-out' at night. Patrick Tobin tells the story of how two senior boys turned up at his house to announce to him, and his wife Margery, that it was 'inconceivable that a married man could successfully run Prior Park.' If that was not discouraging enough perhaps more so was the revelation that boys, of an evening, had taken to ringing up former Christian Brother members of staff to consult them on tactics whereby this alien regime could be subverted. Murmurings occasionally exploded into rather unpleasant acts of indiscipline. On 5 November, prefects threw their ties onto the bonfire; a school hymn practice was met with organised corporate silence; a house safe was burgled; tyres of a car slashed and acid poured onto the bonnet of other staff cars. Perhaps all this nastiness was summed up when a pupil called the Headmaster to his face 'the biggest all-time bastard.'

2nd XI Hockey Squad 2003 / 2004

Back: *Josephine Close, Skye Saker, Lucy Sewell, Sofie Fohlmann, Megan Humphreys, Anna Greene, Hannah Forshaw.* Front: *Marianna Fragapane, Lucy Oatley, Katy Sainsbury, Natalie Dicorato, Nina Spencer, Antonia Robinson, Anna Mee.*

The Prior Park String Quartet, 1986. Nigel Leat, William Turner, Sue Mock and Michael Moorsom are playing.

New arrivals to the Sixth Form. (L to r: Nicola Horstmann, Nicola Bryan, Debbie Cole, Katherine Taylor, Theresa Stickney, Vanessa Bradshaw).

The new girls relax in St Mary's.

To move the school on from all this, a staff team had to be welded together and a common purpose achieved. It needed all the frenetic energy of Patrick Tobin and the wisdom of his choice, on the ever-loyal Sidney Ash's retirement, of Wilfred Hammond as his Deputy Head. Wilfred, a laid-back fell-walking historian from Durham School, was the perfect partner for Tobin. In fact, for all the discontented murmurings of the old brigade, Patrick Tobin was only too anxious to achieve continuity with the best of the past. At his first Speech Day he acknowledged that, with the Christian Brothers leaving, 'an external sign of being a Catholic school' had been lost. He appreciated the Brothers' aim to make Prior Park something 'different', avoiding the snobbishness associated with public schools, and instead forging a friendly community. The challenge to them all now, he believed, was to have a shared purpose in carrying this forward into a new situation for he was convinced that there was an important niche to be filled by such a pastorally-minded caring school community. And the icons of the past were not all hostile to the new regime. Kathy Rowsell, who died at the end of 1983, was such. She had worked for fifty years in the College eventually becoming Housekeeper in the Mansion. As was to be expected, she was passionately loyal to Prior Park and loved its pupils. She lived long enough to see the beginnings of the new regime and her words to Patrick Tobin in one of his darker hours were words of support and reassurance: 'everything will be all right, sir. You'll see!' Meanwhile, as a sign of hope for the future, a daughter Sophie had been born to Patrick and Margery on 30 September 1981 – to become the first child born to a head of Prior Park College.

Despite all this energy the finances did not look good. The College had opened its doors to day pupils who were willing 'to be rooted in a thriving and happy boarding community'. Yet there was a worry about maintaining the strength of that community. Could Prior Park recruit enough boarding pupils? And then there was the delicate question of the quality of new recruits. As Patrick Tobin saw it, the College desperately needed 'an academic transfusion'. Where would that come from? At Prize Giving in May 1983, he was able to announce the beginnings of that revolution which had been so firmly resisted in the past. 'We have girls at Prior Park – all six of them!' The promise was made that by the following year there would be

Some of the first female musicians.

twelve in the Lower Sixth. Now, of course, girls can be introduced to boys' schools for a variety of reasons – to bring in the sorely needed extra cash, to improve academic or civilised standards or to make life easier for families which would like all their young, female as well as male, housed for education in one place. There are all sorts of sensible practical reasons for this widening of intake but experience has shown that to dally with co-education is rarely successful. Life for girls in schools, which are simply boys' schools with female additions, is not a happy one. They can be either idolised or scorned. It is quite clear from conversation with some of the girl pioneers from those early days that their situation was not satisfactory and could not really have continued.

In the end there is no half-way resting place between the single-sex school and full-blooded co-education. So Patrick Tobin tested the waters with both staff and parents. The former seemed to have had more worries about the prospect. Would not the girls distract the boys from their studies? It is interesting how it is always

Two Chairmen of Governors, Colonel R.S.C. Dowden and Mr F.J.F. Lyons enjoy the Mansion terrace.

Jeremy Goulding.

put this way round for rarely is it judged that boys might distract girls. What was discovered amongst parents was that, not only was there 'no great hostility to co-education' but that they were as a whole more open to making the complete change than had been imagined. The Chairman of the Governors, Fergus Lyons, was all for seizing the opportunity. 'Prudence' he judged was 'a luxury Prior Park could not afford'. So, with remarkable speed, the College was headed for full co-education. The establishment of the Priory as the girls' boarding house under Wilfred Hammond's wife, Anne, was a milestone on this journey. Of course reaching the necessary goal of an equal partnership between male and female proved to be a slow process. In such a solidly male world, nothing less than a revolution is required in its leadership. For a long time the meeting of Heads of Houses was still called the Housemasters' Meeting! The growing up process begun in the Tobin era continued under his successor Jeremy Goulding and probably was not near completion until the days of Giles Mercer. By this time the school was a pretty even mix of girls and boys, numbers of female staff had increased, there were both male and female tutors in all houses and women had made significant advances into senior management.

What amidst all this change was going to happen to the religious identity of the College? When two or three are gathered together to consider any Catholic institution, before long there will be an agonising over the preservation of 'Catholic identity'. Patrick Tobin, with an historian's eye, spotted that in 1984 the College could celebrate the 150th anniversary of Bishop Baines first giving Benediction of the Blessed Sacrament from the steps, which he had built before the Mansion. Coming at the time of Speech Day, a clear statement of Catholic continuity could be made by such a celebration. So on 26 May there were Vespers and

Benediction on the Mansion steps. The weather was uncertain so, like many another organiser of May outdoor events, the College hierarchy wavered about the proper venue. Should it be in the Chapel for safety or should the risk be taken of having it outside on the steps? The decision was left for Fr Paul to take at the last minute. By then enclosed beneath the ceremonial canopy, so failing to spot that it had actually started to rain, he took the riskier option and launched the event into blowing rain, a wild wind and a sharp drop in the temperature. The sodden freezing congregation watched apprehensively as the Monstrance, holding the Blessed Sacrament, appeared to be about to be blown from its Throne. The statement thus made about continuing Catholicity acquired a certain ambiguity. Was the faith of Baines, Clifford, Williams and the Christian Brothers about to be blown away by the winds of change?

As the College could not afford to be too 'choosey' about the religious affiliations of its pupils and as it accordingly widened its intake, the number of those, both staff and students, who were Catholics declined. As Abraham had argued with God over how many 'just' men there had to be to save Sodom, so now there were those who pondered on what percentage of Catholics was required to save its religious ethos. Yet the College, like Fr Paul on the steps of the Mansion, chose the riskier option. It decided that the desire of those who were not themselves Roman Catholics to send their young to Prior Park to be part of an overtly Catholic community, constituted not a threat but an opportunity. Maybe the place would not be quite what Baines had meant it to be – a college to supply priests for the Church in the West Country – but then it might fulfil his wider dream of a generous Catholicism reaching out to serve the whole community. In any case the Catholic framework remained firmly in place. The school week centred on the Sunday Mass which combined musical and ceremonial splendour with a touch of populist earthiness and during the week the Mass moved out from the Chapel to be celebrated more simply in the growing number of Houses for both boarding and day pupils. The College's musical tradition was not only continued under Andrew Mock, Richard Dunster-Sigtermans, and Roland Robertson but also developed and enhanced. Sunday-by-Sunday pupils were exposed to the music of the likes of Mozart, Haydn and Schubert, which was washed down with draughts of lusty hymn singing and immoderate waves of incense. They seemed to like this brew and with boys and girls together ministering as Eucharistic Ministers and with girls as well as boys serving at the altar, the liturgy became visibly inclusive, an expression of the nature of this Catholic community.

It soon also became clear that sharp Catholic identity must not be a threat to those members of the College who were not themselves Roman Catholics. Anglicans and Methodists needed to have their own identities positively affirmed. So it came to be that Confirmation candidates from different Christian traditions were able to share most of the preparation together with the Catholics but would also have the opportunity of sitting at the feet of ministers from their own church communities. For some years, the much-loved Vicar of Combe Down, the Revd Jeremy Wordsworth, came to provide an Anglican input. It was therefore a natural development when the College began to welcome not only the Bishop of Clifton to preside over the Catholic Confirmation, but also one of the local Anglican bishops to do the same for his flock. Prior Park's journey takes it, not away from its Catholic roots, but into an ever-deeper commitment to the task of working for Christian unity. Economic necessity may have initially edged it out of a Catholic ghetto into embracing those who were not Catholics but God, as always, moves in a mysterious way, or as Bishop Baines used to say ' Providence

The fire of 1991 as seen from The Circus. Photographed and reproduced by kind permission of Michael Pitts.

leads the way.' When former pupil Cormac Murphy O'Connor came back in 2003, as the Cardinal Archbishop of Westminster, to preside over Speech Day, he seemed to confirm this blend of continuity and development.

Heading for full co-education and committed to a broadening of its religious embrace, Prior Park chose, not the way of safety-first but that of boldness and risk. And, as Patrick Tobin began to win his battles and Jeremy Goulding, a Housemaster from Shrewsbury, who followed him, consolidated all this, the choice seemed to be justified. Of course there continued to be those 'set-backs', which seem to be part and parcel of the College's destiny. The devastating storm of 1990 not only decimated the beloved Rainbow Woods but also threatened to seal Jeremy Goulding and his family into their home, Kent House. But a year later came an even greater test – the second Prior Park fire in August 1991.

Catherine Tomlinson, a pupil at that time, wrote a powerful account of this event, how on a fine summer's afternoon just 'a waft of smoke' was to be seen 'climbing through the Mansion roof'. The people of Bath watched – at first 'with some ease. It seemed so little, so totally controllable – nothing really to worry about.

'But as dusk fell on the city, a blazing building could be seen on the top of the southern hillside. Flames seemed to dance across the roof, destroying everything; they built in strength, overpowering the water jets, overpowering everything. They ripped through the building like dominoes falling, nothing could stop them.

Locals and staff watch in amazement as firefighters tackle the blaze.

Firemen at work. With the kind permission of the *Bath Chronicle*.

Firemen at work. With the kind permission of the *Bath Chronicle*.

Fire damage to the Academy Hall.

An aerial shot taken and reproduced by the kind permission of Mr A Wilson. Damage to the John Wood Chapel can clearly be seen to the left.

The Bursar, Paul Turfery, takes a look at the damage to the Academy Hall.

Above the building, clouds of thick, hot, grey-black smoke had billowed out, sweeping through the hundreds of onlookers gazing in silent, horrified awe at the uncontrollable fire. There was a general feeling of devastation. One watched the magnificent architecture of the Academy Hall and the John Wood Chapel crumble and melt as another floor collapsed, burying a little more history each time.'
All this she wrote 'not only left the physical aspects of the College gutted but also the souls of many of the people of Bath who watched history burn and fade away before them.'

Coming when it did, as the College was dragging itself out of danger, this disaster could easily have been fatal. Not only was the magnificent heart of the College, the Mansion, destroyed but also more practically there went with it all the administrative offices, Sister McPeake's flat and surgery, and the increasingly important music department. And all this had happened just a week or two before the new academic year was due to begin.

Scaffolding goes up in preparation for re-building.

It was only the resilience and gritty determination of the Headmaster Jeremy Goulding and the Bursar, Paul Turfery, which saved the day. Immediately after the fire they sat down with the architect and devised ways of bringing the school back on time for the autumn term and making its continued life possible. Mercifully the kitchens and refectory in the basement of the Mansion escaped the fire and could be sealed off to continue in business. The school was thus enabled to march forward on its stomach. As for the Headmaster's study, the secretariat, and the Bursary, they had to be banished to the edges of the top playing field to inhabit cricket pavilions while the staff were packed up there into a temporary hut for a Common Room. It was a very testing time for all; but the goal was achieved. Boys and girls came back at the proper time and then school was up and running.

Inevitably as time went by and the necessarily painstaking work on Mansion continued, a certain weariness descended as staff struggled with these make-shift arrangements. Gazing at the Mansion encased in scaffolding and a vast plastic jacket, the young poet Katherine Green saw
'Beauty and grace, lying dormant,
Waiting to be woken and set free.
Like an exquisite bird in a cage,
Its cries unheard,
Silent to human ears.'
So students joined with staff to long for the moment when the bird would be *'cast away.*
Into its flight of freedom
To display its dignity and pride, once again.'

However there was the opening of the new Sixth Form Centre and Theatre to be looked forward to. This was the generous gift of Cameron Mackintosh. Headmaster and Bursar drove the work on this forward, knowing that it would provide just that extra bit of space and become a sign of hope for the future. So it was that the donor was able, in the presence of the inspirer of his dreams, the writer of *Salad Days*, Julian Slade to open the Theatre and dedicate it to him. Further relief in this time of hardship was provided by the new astro-turf all-weather pitch, which was sorely needed by the hockey players who were becoming increasingly skilled and successful under the expert coaching of Allan Hall. And then of course at last came that triumphant re-opening of the Mansion, restored, but, as after the first fire, also enhanced. Not only had the plasterers with infinite care and great ingenuity reassembled the mouldings in the Academy Hall but also the somewhat

Sir Cameron Mackintosh, Julian Slade, Lionel Bart and Christopher Ash pictured at the opening of the Slade Theatre in 1993.

Julian Slade unveils a plaque at the opening of the Slade Theatre.

grotty attics of the Mansion, which once upon a time had housed those Irish maids, were transformed into a fine new Music department. The old was enhanced and the new was advanced.

Here history ends and the present begins. The old continues to be enhanced and the new advanced as Jeremy Goulding and Giles Mercer follow the pioneering Patrick Tobin while, out at Cricklade, Gerry Hoburn has ensured that the Prep School shares in this new flourishing of Baines's dream. As chairmen of governors, Fergus Lyons, Ronnie Dowden and Chris Davey have led a devoted and increasingly diverse governing body with vision and vigour. The new era was perhaps formally marked by the purchase of the freehold of Prior Park from the Christian Brothers in July 1999. What has been inherited has been improved. Under the guidance of the hardworking and ever cheerful Bursar, Captain Charles Freeman, the boys' boarding houses have been refurbished, the girls' boarding house, the Priory, extended and for day girls a new house, All Saints, built. All this was more than necessary, for the 232 pupils whom Tobin inherited have become 540. Instead of having to go out to the highways and byways in search of recruits, the College is now faced with more demand for places than it can satisfy. And it is not just a matter of numbers; it is the quality of the school's life, which has been enriched. Academic achievements are many and impressive. These are the result not just of the seriousness and application, which the demands of an endless regime of examinations require, but of a growing intellectual buzz and excitement which are manifest in a revival of formal debating and annual participation in the local schools' United Nations. For several years now the College has won acclaim for its creative poetry writing. The extraordinary thing about so many young people today is how talented they are and how they manage to juggle the demands of these many talents. That hulking be-muddied member of the rugby pack is likely to be singing a solo at Mass the following day or dancing with remarkable elegance and grace in the chorus of the latest musical.

Denis and Jenny Clarke with Martin Woodhouse, Jon-Col Shin, Sebastien Allen and Rupert Whittaker in their sitting room in Roche House in 1986.

Dr and Mrs Mercer at the Leavers' Ball.

Wilfred Hammond and pupils preparing to set off on an expedition in 1986.

The repertoire of games has somewhat broadened, so that along with rugby, hockey, netball and cricket, athletics, tennis and cross-country running now have a higher profile. Sporting activities are no longer the exclusive preserve of an elite; they are for all to enjoy. At every level of the school Prior Park's tradition of drama and music has been developed. Theatre studies are now taught as an academic subject, dance is taken seriously and involves both boys and girls. Under the guidance of the head of department, and with the assistance of many members of staff such as Richard Wells, the number of productions every year has increased and ranges from great popular musicals to demanding Shakespearean plays such as *Lear* and *Othello*. Choral music of a high standard continues to be an essential part of the Sunday Masses and there has been an advance in instrumental playing, orchestral work and the development of lively jazz bands.

All these activities make for a vibrant life but beyond activities there is the quality of community life, the sort of place, which Prior Park is. Something of the old determination to be a bit different, to avoid snobbishness and those deadly school hierarchies, to be a friendly informal community, to be a place where everyone can feel at ease and accepted – something of all this has stuck. A culture inimical to bullying has been fashioned and one created which treats looking after one another as natural. In those most testing times when students experience sickness of a parent or even bereavement, the sense of solidarity and practical compassion is powerful. It continues to move out beyond the school community in the work done by Prior Concern, in the participation of pupils in the City's Soup Run for the homeless, and wider afield in the Gap Year project in Tanzanian schools, which provides leavers with opportunities for service. The fashioning of this culture is the result both of the hard work and determination of its teaching staff in which the leadership of the Deputy Head, Denis Clarke has proved decisive, and the commitment of students. But perhaps Ralph Allen's amazing gift has a part to play for it is still 'a place with a view.' The young can still stand on Baines's steps and gaze, and wonder. And that touches the heart of the Catholic matter – the care for one another which springs from the ability to stop, to gaze and to wonder at 'that which no greater can be conceived.'

The Governing Body of 1998. Captain Charles Freeman, John Mill, Chris Davy, John Evans, Michael Thesiger, Bernard Kelly, Andrew Pitt, Dr Finola Roche, Fr Tom Gunning, Sr Andrea le Guevel, David Corrigan, Andrew Owen, Dr Giles Mercer, Rear Admiral Mike Vallis, Colonel Ronnie Dowden, Alan Cooper, Gerry Hobern.

Bibliography

As mentioned in the Introduction my primary sources have been:
Prior Park School Magazines starting around 1887.
The Bath Chronicle for the late eighteenth century and the nineteenth century.
Various items in the Clifton Diocesan Archive.
Catholic Record Society – *Catholicism in Bath Vol. 1*, Ed J Anthony Williams.
Gordon Riot Documents and the Journal of Peter Augustine Baines.

The written recollections of former staff and pupils, which include:
Reminiscences of Mr James Kavanagh, L L Guibara. Serialised in Prior Park Magazine 1887.
Recollections of Kevin Tyndall.
Memories of Br John Greenan.
The Flutes of Autumn, Peter Levi. Harvill Press Limited 1983.
Portrait of a Putney Pud, Patrick Tobin. The Memoir Club 2004.

Earlier histories of Prior Park:
Prior Park, J S Roche. Burns Oates 1931.
Prior Park – Its History and Description, Bryan Little. Burleigh Press 1975.

Background:
Bath and Rome – The Living Link, J Anthony Williams. TRUEXpress, Oxford 1963.
Life of John Henry Newman, Wilfrid Ward 1912.
Rosmini: Priest, Philosopher and Patriot, Claude Leetham. Longmans Green and Co. 1957.
Life and Times of Bishop Ullathorne, Cuthbert Butler. Burns Oates 1925.
The English Catholic Community 1570–1850, John Bossy. DLT 1975.
More Roman than Rome – English Catholicism in the Nineteenth Century, J Derek Homes. Burns Oates 1978.
The Victorian Church, Owen Chadwick. Adam and Charles Black 1966.